The Ypsilanti Perry Preschool Project was made possible by a grant from the Office of Education, U.S. Department of Health, Education, & Welfare, through the Ypsilanti, Michigan, Public School System. Funds granted by the Spencer Foundation of Chicago and the Carnegie Corporation of New York made it possible to undertake follow-up data collection and data analysis. The statements made and the views expressed are solely the responsibility of the authors.

HIGH/SCOPE
EDUCATIONAL RESEARCH FOUNDATION
Ypsilanti, Michigan

Monographs of the
High/Scope Educational Research Foundation
Number Three

THE YPSILANTI PERRY PRESCHOOL PROJECT

Preschool Years and Longitudinal Results Through Fourth Grade

D.P. Weikart, J.T. Bond and
J.T. McNeil
High/Scope Educational Research Foundation

with commentary by

E. Kuno Beller
Temple University

Robert D. Hess
Stanford University

Library of Congress Cataloging in Publication Data

Weikart, David P
 Ypsilanti Perry preschool project.

 (Monographs of the High/Scope Educational
Research Foundation; no. 3 ISSN 0149-242X)
  Bibliography: p.
  1. Education, Preschool—Michigan—Ypsilanti.
2. Education, Primary—Michigan—Ypsilanti.
I. Bond, J.T., joint author. II. McNeil, J.T., joint au-
thor. III. Title. IV. Series: High/Scope Educational
Research Foundation. Monographs of the High/Scope
Educational Research Foundation; no.3.
LB 1140.2.W438   372.21   77-92916

ISBN 0-931114-02-0

Contents

Tables & Figures

Tables

Figures

Figures (continued)

Acknowledgments

Conducting a longitudinal study of this magnitude has required the cooperation and sustained commitment of many staff members, organizations, and families over many years. This particular study has been blessed with project families who have remained involved in spite of minimal benefit to themselves; with staff who have recognized the service to children that preschool provides and who have given liberally and willingly of themsleves; with teachers, school principals, local and county administrators, and a Board of Education in the Ypsilanti schools that have encouraged and supported the data collection even when it was not convenient for them to do so; and with two funding organizations which have provided long-term support when it was most needed—the Spencer Foundation (1972 to 1974) and the Carnegie Corporation (1975 to 1978). Without the direct assistance of all of these people and groups the project could not have continued.

Within the High/Scope Foundation, data collection and analyses have been provided by various staff members over the years. Ronald Wiegerink, Dennis Deloria, Robert Rentfrow, John Larson, and Donald Sommerfeld have supervised field staff and maintained data collection quality. Bob Hanvey and Nancy Naylor have taken responsibility for data management and solved the long-term problems of storing and retrieving complex information collected over many years. In addition, many other staff members have assisted in the actual data collection on a part-time basis, lending their interest and enthusiasm to the project as each year's problems were resolved. Without such dedicated staff this longitudinal project could not have been carried out.

David P. Weikart
Ypsilanti, Michigan
February 1977

Introduction

The Ypsilanti Perry Preschool Project is a study of the long-term effects, on a group of disadvantaged children, of a preschool education program operated in the Ypsilanti, Michigan, school system. The preschool program attempted to build the cognitive skills and attitudes these children would need to compete successfully in school. The primary social-service goal of the project was to prevent adolescent delinquency and school dropout among these so-called "high risk" children.

It was not a simple matter to initiate a public preschool program in 1962. State educational policies as well as local school traditions did not encourage such activities. The professional resources needed to support a preschool program tended to be in university lab schools and were not readily accessible to the public schools. Yet the potential of early education for the disadvantaged* seemed obvious enough. The slow movement toward social change which began in the late fifties produced a hospitable climate; and eventually, because of this climate, there were changes in the rules and regulations of the Michigan education system which cleared away the legal and administrative obstacles. After two years of planning, the Perry Project was launched in October 1962, four months after Susan Gray initiated a preschool research project in Murphysboro, Tennessee (Gray and Klaus, 1970) and two months before Martin Deutsch began a preschool project in New York City (Deutsch, 1962). Enthusiasm for preschool education hit its high mark in 1965 when National Head Start was launched to prepare disadvantaged children for entrance into kindergarten on a par with their middle-class peers.

From the perspective of the seventies it is difficult to imagine the social and educational matrix of 1962 that generated and controlled the Perry Project. So many practices and conditions we take for granted today were simply not part of the realm of consideration at that time: frequent participation by parents in educational decision-making, extensive use of computers as tools for analysis of data, acceptance of schooling for children whose mental age was below six years, large-scale national educational research projects, special focus on the needs of disadvantaged children, and mandatory special-education legislation at the national and state levels. In order to understand the research focus and the educational orientation of the Perry Project, then, it is useful to review the historical situation within which the project took shape.

The situation in the early 1960's was marked by a turning away from the "creative" and humanistic emphasis of the progressive movement in education. The Russian Sputnik's dramatic ascent into space had created a sudden commitment to the three R's in the hope of adding science and

---

*At the time the rather stilted expression was "culturally deprived." While the fact that the families of these children had little money and few educational opportunities was recognized, the implications of these conditions were overlooked by most professionals. Not until the seventies did the more realistic terms "disadvantaged" and "economically disadvantaged" become common usage.

engineering skills to the capacities of the American student. Bester's *Why Johnny Can't Read* was in vogue. A major topic of concern in the educational circles of the day was how to counter the problem of juvenile delinquency. It was believed that the achievement problems of minority or lower-class children could be solved by the proper application of firm discipline by the teacher and hard work by the child. Classes in schools were large and relatively uncomplicated by outside consultation or special federal or state projects for low-achieving students. Salaries started at $4200 a year for the teacher just out of college, and there were plenty of teaching jobs. Principals ran their buildings without interference from unions, parents, or central administration.

Public education handled its "problem learners" chiefly in one of three ways: (1) referral to outside agencies to adjust the child for better behavior and achievement, (2) referral to the special-services staff of the school to counsel the child and family or to "hold" the youngster in a special-education class, or (3) retention of the child in grade by "failing" him, in an effort to help the child learn the skills and behaviors appropriate to one grade level before advancing to the next.

Each of these methods had severe shortcomings. Near Ypsilanti, for example, the local psychiatric hospital would accept referrals only for those children who were "verbal enough to benefit" (defined as above average IQ) from standard therapeutic treatment; and the hospital accepted appointments only during the working day, which meant that the family had to have two cars and one nonworking parent to permit scheduling of long-term treatment. These policies effectively disqualified many children from low-income families.

Special services within the schools were similarly hamstrung by a traditional short-sightedness (though in Ypsilanti, a school system of only 7000 students, the addition of 40 special-service staff in three years clearly indicated a recognition of educational problems and a willingness to act on the part of the schools). Learning problems were usually perceived to be within the child and family and rarely within the school or instructional model. It was the child who must change, not the curriculum. Further, once the child was identified as being in need of special education, the regular classroom teacher frequently refused, in a variety of subtle ways, to have anything more to do with him, saying, in effect, I'm not trained in special education, I'm not being paid the premium salary to cope with such problems, and I don't have the small class apparently required by such youngsters nor all of that fancy equipment.

Children unable to learn at the standard rate were seen simply as failures. The major remedy of choice was to require students to repeat grades until they learned the necessary skills. This practice produced, in Ypsilanti, the outlandish result of approximately 50% of all ninth-graders being from one to five years behind in grade, and a 50% dropout rate with legal school-leaving occurring for some youngsters as early as seventh grade. This pattern was probably not significantly different from that of any other middle-class/working-class community in the state.

In the late fifties, the special-services staff of the Ypsilanti schools (of which David Weikart was then head) and several innovative principals attempted to introduce some modifications in the system's position vis-a-vis low-achieving students. For example, a series of curriculum meetings was held to present basic information on student performance as measured by standardized tests, on the systematic retention of low-achieving students, and on the close relationship of these issues to social class. Out of these meetings came a major observation which has a very contemporary ring: the schools were unprepared for change. The reaction of the participants to one meeting will illustrate. The focus of the meeting was individual school achievement data by grade, drawn from a ten-year record of standardized testing. The principals from each building in the system gathered around a long conference table to listen to the presentation. One by one they responded vividly as the meeting proceeded. One principal stood up and walked to the window, smoking his pipe, and showed no further awareness of the group; another abruptly pushed his chair back from the table and crossed his arms and legs; and several others began a whispered conversation about other topics. The outcome of the meeting was an agreement that no principal should be prevented from doing what was "best for the children" by limits on his power to retain a child more than two years in the same grade—the only proposal the group even allowed to be introduced.

We like to think that such unresponsiveness is a thing of the past. But when we look closely at such "innovations" as behavioral objectives and programmed learning, it becomes difficult to avoid the suspicion that the policy of "no change" is still entrenched—for these are devices to alter the *child*, to adjust *him* to the curriculum rather than change the procedures of schooling so that curriculum becomes more responsive to the *child's* requirements.

The impetus for the Ypsilanti Perry Preschool Project, then, was the recognition that the local school system, certainly representative of the times, was unable or unwilling to promise even minor reforms to permit low-achieving children some success in school. The failure of the school administration and teachers to adjust the curriculum was seen by the special-services staff as a factor contributing to juvenile delinquency, to the high referral rate of minority and lower-class children to special services for "treatment," and to the high retention-in-grade and dropout rate of these children. Since the schools would not, or could not, change, the plan devised by Weikart, his special-services staff and the principals was to equip high-risk children with improved abilities to cope with the demands of schooling. This was to be done before the children entered school, because a preschool program would be relatively unencumbered by administrative red tape and district-wide curricular requirements. The staff could concentrate on developing a program that truly served the children.

At the time the project began, there was no reason to believe that preschool could alter either intelligence or achievement test patterns, though such alterations were certainly hoped for, especially the intellectual gains. Had academic gains been the focus, the program might have evolved toward an academic training model and eventually into a didactic behavioral system. Instead, the staff elected to focus on developing the capacity of the children to wrest education from a reluctant school system. To this end, home teaching was made a regular part of the program, because the parents would of course be involved with the youngsters long after preschool. It was the hope of the special-services staff that a preschool program that worked, combined with parental involvement, would help to prevent juvenile delinquency and thereby give these children a chance to succeed in life.

The basic research question of the project was this: Would the children who had the preschool experience be more successful in school than a nonparticipating and randomly assigned control group? Interim success was defined as intellectual and achievement growth and regular grade-level placement versus special-education placement. Long-term success was defined as a reduced dropout rate and a reduction in juvenile delinquency.

The various purposes of the project can now be summed up briefly. The project set out to develop a methodology whereby children seen as high-risk in terms of successfully completing an elementary and secondary education could "beat" the system which would not accommodate to them. The effects of the preschool program developed for these children were to be compared with the consequences of no preschool for a control group of similarly disadvantaged children; and this comparison was to be done on a long-term basis, with periodic assessment of the children's progress through adolescence. Although a specific curriculum was to be evolved along with specific procedures such as home teaching, this was to be a study of preschool versus no preschool and not one of curriculum. The hope was that early educational intervention would produce a permanent intellectual capacity at a critical period* in the child's development sufficient to prevent any backsliding, at least through the schooling period.

Once the project was conceptualized, the state of Michigan was contacted for permission to operate the program. This step was essential since the state, in 1959, had altered pupil-reimbursement procedures to permit services from birth through 25 years of age to children diagnosed as mentally retarded. State provisions had existed earlier for physically handicapped children, but inclusion of the mentally handicapped opened the door to minority and lower-class children who were not mentally handicapped in any organic sense but simply met the criteria defined by the school system. Meetings with the state special-education consultant determined that the program could be operated and reimbursed as long as qualified teachers could be found to insure quality education. "Qualified" was defined as being certified in three areas: preschool, regular elementary, and educable mentally handicapped. The obstacles to finding such teachers seemed insurmountable. In 1962, teachers with any type of

---

*The work of Scott (1962) and others with animals had popularized the idea of critical periods, and this concept was considered by many psychologists to be relevant to human intellectual and academic development.

A deficit theory of development was implicit throughout the early years of the project. This position was in agreement with the standard educational theory of the time and, indeed, is still adhered to by many educators. The difference in outlook of the Perry Project can be seen in its assumption that the way for disadvantaged children to gain abilities they lack is through an experienced-based rather than a didactic program.

certificate were in short supply, public-school teachers certified in pre-school education were all but unheard of, and teachers certified for work with the mentally handicapped were being offered premium salaries. After a four-month search, however, four teachers were found who had both elementary and special-education certification. They agreed to attend summer school at local universities to pick up additional preschool courses, and the preschool opened in the fall of 1962.

Application to the National Institute of Mental Health for research money was unsuccessful, so the project functioned during its first year with in-house research support. In a public school, that meant doing the research work with whoever could be persuaded to donate time and energy to meet the deadlines. The following year, with the aid and encouragement of Dr. Nicholas Georgiday and Dr. John Porter of the Michigan Department of Education, an application was submitted to the Cooperative Educational Research Branch of the U.S. Office of Education. To the surprise and pleasure of the staff, a four-year, $120,000 grant was awarded, and the project became one of the few public school programs ever to be awarded such a grant.

Perhaps one of the most difficult things for the staff to face in the beginning was the skepticism of professionals in early childhood and special education. The confidential advice from the director of one major institutional teacher-training program was, "Don't be foolish. A child must achieve a mental age of six years before it is worth offering an educational program." State special-education consultants were genuinely alarmed about the project, because the revisions of the state code imagined consulting services to parents, not public-school classrooms for children. The fact that the project was being developed and directed by public-school personnel without guidance from a university staff also raised some eyebrows. Fortunately the Perry Project staff were hardy enough to withstand such doubts and to move ahead to resolve a wide range of initial legal and financial problems. The major task that remained, and a formidable one at that, was to develop a curricular approach that would serve the goals of the project.

The principal research projects on preschool education up to the early sixties had been conducted on university preschools set up for the children of academics. The major reviews of the literature, such as Fuller (1960), focused on studies of general child development with emphasis on social-emotional growth and little reference to cognitive development or language acquisition. A major pioneering experimental study had been conducted by Kirk (1958) for children with various handicapping conditions, including a mildly retarded group of children who today would be labeled economically disadvantaged. Prior to Kirk's study, the major preschool research effort had been that of the staff and students of the Iowa Child Welfare Research Station (Skeels, Updegraph, Wellman, and Williams, 1938; Skodak and Skeels, 1949; and Wellman, 1945).

The child-development theory and the educational philosophy for preschool practice at that time were derived from Freudian psychology. The focus was principally on social adjustment and the mother-child relationship (e.g., Jersild and Fite, 1939). Piaget's work, which was to influence the program so deeply, was hardly known in this country. The

Piaget bandwagon did not really begin to roll until the late sixties.*

The Cognitively Oriented Curriculum evolved by stages, or rather by upheavals. Initially, the idea was that a group of teachers and researchers would work together to establish a curriculum geared to the skills required to function in a school environment. It was difficult to transform this goal into a daily plan of operation. Weekly meetings, lesson plans, recognition of teacher knowledge, and capacity to serve as a valuable resource were all difficult for the research staff to accept. Child-development theory, data-collection plans, and research restrictions were equally hard for teachers to accept. It often seemed that elaborate charades were enacted to avoid the group decisions that had to be made. Group cooperation was a difficult skill to achieve. About six weeks into the project, with most of the staff concentrating on their own survival in a group setting, the children became increasingly restless in the classroom. Our special new brand of preschool programming was not functioning! The stress on the teachers was great—with morning classes at the neighborhood center, afternoon home-teaching assignments, and demands for data collection from the research staff. One day an aggressive four-year-old tossed a folding chair across the classroom in frustration. That afternoon the teaching/research staff planning session had a seriousness of focus that had been missing in prior meetings. The educational program was launched for the staff as well as the children; and now something more powerful than fear of self-exposure began to take hold, to mold the staff into a unified body dedicated first and foremost to the betterment of children's lives.

One issue that affected the development of the curriculum for many years was the question of the "value" of teachers versus the "value" of research staff. Who was going to have the final say on the different phases of work? At first the teachers desired and appreciated input from the research staff on the issues of content, theory, and curriculum development. However, the research staff frequently found the concerns and even the goals of the teaching staff foreign to their own interpretation of the project. Who was to decide, to control, to direct? Over the years the project lost several key teachers and research staff over this issue. As the teacher group gained experience, they became increasingly independent of the research staff and less willing to discount their classroom experience and knowledge in order to accept the theoretical dicta of the research staff. The job of the director was to blend the practical and the theoretical inputs so that the program would reflect a true synthesis of these positions and not just a compromise worked out to prevent a stalemate. The Cognitively Oriented Curriculum as presently constituted is in fact such a synthesis of theory and practice. It is precisely because of this struggle to effect a realistic application of Piagetian theory that the Perry Preschool Project staff was able to achieve the encouraging results reported in this monograph.

---

*Our experience in obtaining information about Piagetian theory might illustrate the point. A search was made to find a consultant within the state who could provide the project staff with a seminar series on Piagetian theory. After discussions with several universities and institutes, a recent Yale Ph.D. graduate was found who had both heard of Piaget and had actually done enough reading to lead the seminar. From the vantage of the seventies it is difficult to realize that in 1963 few people, even at major universities, had heard of Piaget and that a program would be widely criticized for departing from the Freudian psycho-social-development orientation.

I Experimental design

Overview

The Ypsilanti Perry Preschool Project was among the first of many innovative preschool programs for economically disadvantaged children which appeared in the early 1960's. From 1962 through 1967, 123 academically high-risk preschool-age children participated in the project. This group comprised five successive "waves" of children who entered the project one year apart. Approximately equal numbers of children in each wave belonged to independent experimental and control groups. Experimental-group children attended preschool when they were three and four years old; the children in the control group had no intervention other than annual testing. Both groups entered the same public schools at age five, and no further intervention has taken place since, except for periodic data collection.

The major assumption underlying the Perry Project was that children from low-income families who scored low on psychometric tests of intelligence at three years of age would benefit from attending preschool; many cognitive and social benefits were expected during preschool, through elementary school and into adulthood.

The basic experiment contrasted children who attended preschool with children who did not. Other *independent variables*—sex, initial child measures, and home background—were included in the design both to increase the precision with which treatment effects could be isolated and to provide information on the relative importance of other factors in the child's experience. The *dependent variables* considered in this report include standardized tests of academic aptitude and achievement, teachers' ratings of children's attitudes and behavior, indices of school success, and mothers' descriptions of home environment.

Project families were selected from the population living in the attendance area of Perry Elementary School in Ypsilanti, Michigan. The sampling universe was further delimited by selecting children whose scores on the Stanford-Binet Intelligence Scale were within a particular range and who were from families of low socio-economic status (SES). Approximately one half of the sample was assigned to the experimental treatment: two years of preschool and weekly home visits by teachers with mother and child. The remaining children constituted a control group which received the same testing as the experimental group but did not attend preschool or receive home visits. Unlike that of many other longitudinal studies, the Perry Project's sample attrition has been slight; for example, of 123 children in the total sample, only one child could not be located during spring 1973 data collection.

Replication

Five pairs of experimental and control groups were used in five replications of the basic experiment from 1962 to 1967. Replicating the experiment with relatively small numbers of children (approximately 25 each time) served two purposes. First, it reduced the operating scale and cost of the experiment to manageable proportions. Second, it guarded against the possibility that unusual circumstances in any given year might distort the findings.

In this report, each group of children involved in successive replications of the experiment will be referred to as a *wave*[1] and given a number from 0 through 4 to designate its position in the sequence of replications. Table 1 indicates the date at which each wave of children was enrolled in the project, the number of children in each treatment group, and the stepwise progression of waves from preschool through fourth grade.

Table 1 also compares the longitudinal coverage of this report with that of the previous report, *Longitudinal Results of the Ypsilanti Perry Preschool Project* (Weikart, Deloria, Lawser and Wiegerink, 1970). That report was limited by the fact that longitudinal findings for kindergarten through third grade were based upon partial data:

- Preschool data—all Waves (0 through 4)
- Kindergarten data—Waves 0, 1, 2, and 3
- First grade data—Waves 0, 1, 2
- Second grade data—Waves 0 and 1
- Third grade data—Wave 0 only

This situation is remedied in the present report, which extends the longitudinal study through fourth grade using data collected on all waves.

One inconsistency in the design is apparent in Table 1: Wave 0 children entered the project as four-year-olds and the Wave 0 experimental group attended only one year of preschool. Originally Wave 0 children were included as "senior preschoolers" to Wave 1 three-year-olds in order to obtain the educational advantage of interactions among older and younger children. Although Wave 0 does not represent a formal replication of the experiment, the concurrent and longitudinal outcomes of the experimental treatment among Wave 0 children are strikingly similar to the effects for Waves 1 through 4 (see chapter II). This seems to justify the decision made here and in the 1970 Perry Report to treat Wave 0 as a "practical replication" of the experiment.

For purposes of analysis, data obtained on Wave 0 children during their one year of preschool will be considered *entering-year data* and grouped with data collected on children in Waves 1 through 4 during their first year of preschool. Wave 0 will be "missing" in analyses of *second-year data* which were obtained on children in the other waves. This grouping of data by waves is illustrated in Table 2. The major data-collection points were fall entering year and every spring thereafter. The following notation will be used in the remainder of this report when referring to specific data-collection points:

---

[1]A wave is defined as one group of subjects in a series of replications in which all major aspects of a study (i.e., sample characteristics, design, treatment, and measures) are held constant for each replication. A wave is a special instance of a cohort, a term which refers to the temporal sequencing of groups but does not imply that the essential research dimensions are held constant.

Table 1

Annual Grade Status of Waves Through Fourth Grade

WAVE	GROUP	N	MEAN AGE AT ENTRY (MONTHS)	SCHOOL YEAR									
				1970 Report[1]					Present Report				
				1962-63	1963-64	1964-65	1965-66	1966-67	1967-68	1968-69	1969-70	1970-71	1971-72
WAVE 0	EXP	13	52.8	PRESCHOOL 1ST YEAR	KINDERGARTEN	1ST GRADE	2ND GRADE	3RD GRADE	4TH GRADE				
	CON	15	50.7										
WAVE 1	EXP	8	40.2	PRESCHOOL 1ST YEAR	PRESCHOOL 2ND YEAR	KINDERGARTEN	1ST GRADE	2ND GRADE	3RD GRADE	4TH GRADE			
	CON	9	39.4										
WAVE 2	EXP	12	40.2		PRESCHOOL 1ST YEAR	PRESCHOOL 2ND YEAR	KINDERGARTEN	1ST GRADE	2ND GRADE	3RD GRADE	4TH GRADE		
	CON	14	40.0										
WAVE 3	EXP	13	38.9			PRESCHOOL 1ST YEAR	PRESCHOOL 2ND YEAR	KINDERGARTEN	1ST GRADE	2ND GRADE	3RD GRADE	4TH GRADE	
	CON	14	39.3										
WAVE 4	EXP	12	40.2				PRESCHOOL 1ST YEAR	PRESCHOOL 2ND YEAR	KINDERGARTEN	1ST GRADE	2ND GRADE	3RD GRADE	4TH GRADE
	CON	13	38.5										

[1]Weikart, Deloria, Lawser, and Wiegerink, 1970

	FEY	(fall entering year)
Preschool:	SEY	(spring entering year)
	S2Y	(spring second year)

	SKG	(spring kindergarten)
	S1G	(spring first grade)
Elementary:	S2G	(spring second grade)
	S3G	(spring third grade)
	S4G	(spring fourth grade)

The sample

The Perry Preschool Project was undertaken in Ypsilanti, Michigan, whose current population is 30,000 (city and township: 63,000). Located 30 miles west of Detroit in southern Michigan's transportation and industrial corridor, Ypsilanti is a microcosm of large midwestern cities. The economic base of the community is diverse and its population heterogeneous. While the 18,000 students who attend Eastern Michigan University are a prominent element in the life of the community, the resident population is predominantly working class. The city and township employ some 23,000 persons in over 60 industries (primarily automotive, plastics, modular homes, and paper manufacturing).

When the project began in 1962, few members of Ypsilanti's black population (25% of total) had achieved middle-class status. Most black heads of households had migrated from the southern states. Many worked in unskilled service occupations in neighboring Ann Arbor. Virtually all lived in the southwest section of the city, primarily in the Perry Elementary School attendance area. Ten years later, the majority of black families still reside on the south side of town and remain predominantly working class.

A decision was made to select project families from among those living in the Perry Elementary School attendance area because their children seemed most in need of early educational support, as judged by the poor academic performance of children at Perry School when compared with their peers in the community at large (see the 1970 Perry Report). The sampling universe was further delimited by identifying among these generally "high risk" children those who seemed least likely to succeed in school. For this purpose, two eligibility criteria were employed: family socio-economic status (SES) and child's performance on the Stanford-Binet Intelligence Scale.

Socio-economic status

In order to determine the specific characteristics of the Perry Elementary School attendance-area population, a questionnaire was administered to the approximately 300 families with children attending Perry School by classroom teachers during parent-teacher conferences in May, 1962. Parents who did not attend these conferences were interviewed in their

Table 2

Wave Grouping of Data for Analysis

DATA COLLECTION POINTS

WAVE	FEY, SEY	S2Y	SKG	S1G	S2G	S3G	S4G
WAVE 0	PRESCHOOL 1ST YEAR		KINDER-GARTEN	1ST GRADE	2ND GRADE	3RD GRADE	4TH GRADE
WAVE 1	PRESCHOOL 1ST YEAR	PRESCHOOL 2ND YEAR	KINDER-GARTEN	1ST GRADE	2ND GRADE	3RD GRADE	4TH GRADE
WAVE 2	PRESCHOOL 1ST YEAR	PRESCHOOL 2ND YEAR	KINDER-GARTEN	1ST GRADE	2ND GRADE	3RD GRADE	4TH GRADE
WAVE 3	PRESCHOOL 1ST YEAR	PRESCHOOL 2ND YEAR	KINDER-GARTEN	1ST GRADE	2ND GRADE	3RD GRADE	4TH GRADE
WAVE 4	PRESCHOOL 1ST YEAR	PRESCHOOL 2ND YEAR	KINDER-GARTEN	1ST GRADE	2ND GRADE	3RD GRADE	4TH GRADE

NOTE: Shaded areas indicate data points analyzed in the 1970 Perry Report; all data points are analyzed in the present report.

homes during the same month. Similar information was collected during this period from parents registering their children for kindergarten at Erickson Elementary School, an all-white school located in a middle-class residential section of the Ypsilanti Public School District. Data on these two groups, together with comparable data obtained from parents of children who entered the Perry Preschool Project in the fall of 1962, are presented in Table 3. Comparisons among the three groups show large and consistent differences in socio-economic status. Families with children in Erickson School placed substantially higher on class-sensitive factors than families from the Perry School area. Perry Project families evidenced consistently lower status on these factors than Perry School families in general.

Socio-economic eligibility was determined by an SES rating adapted from an existing index (Deutsch, 1962) and computed from data obtained in initial interviews using the Perry Demographic Questionnaire. This measure of SES included the following three components:

- *Occupation* of father (or of mother if no father was living in the home) on a four-point scale:
  - 1 = unskilled or unemployed
  - 2 = semiskilled
  - 3 = skilled
  - 4 = professional
- *Education* (years) completed by parents (an average of the two, or the mother's education if no father was living in the home)
- *Density* in the home, defined as the number of rooms (kitchen and bathroom included; shared bath counted as one-half) divided by the number of people living in the home

Scores on the SES index were computed by the following formula:

$$SES = \frac{Education}{{}^{s}Ed} + \frac{Occupation}{{}^{s}Oc} + \frac{½\,Density}{{}^{s}D}$$

The denominators in this equation are the Perry School population standard deviations on the variables in question. Substitution of standard deviations obtained in the original survey produced the following working formula:

$$SES = 1/2\,(Education) + 2\,(Occupation) + 2\,(Density)$$

A score of 11 points on the SES index was adopted as the upper limit for project eligibility. It is our impression that black families living in Ypsilanti at or below this SES level are comparable to poor, inner-city black families in most northern industrial cities.

Stanford-Binet performance

The second eligibility criterion for Perry Project children was that they score between 50 and 85 on the Stanford-Binet Intelligence Scale. The Binet was used because of its ability to predict success in school (i.e., the

Table 3

1962 Demographic-SES Data:
Perry and Erickson School Attendance Areas and Project Subsample

Variable	Erickson School N = 148	Total Perry School N = 277	Perry Preschool Subsample[1] N = 45
MOTHER:			
Average age	32	35	31
Average years of education	12.4	10.1	9.2
% working (full or part time)	15%	60%	20%
Average occupational level[2]	2.8	1.4	1.0
% born in South	22%	77%	80%
% educated in South	17%	53%	48%
FATHER:			
% fathers living in the home	100%	63%	48%
Average age	35	40	35
Average years of education	13.4	9.4	8.3
Average occupational level[2]	3.3	1.6	1.1
FAMILY AND HOME:			
Average SES rating	16.4	11.5	8.2
Average number of children	3.1	3.9	4.5
% on welfare	0%	30%	58%
% home ownership	85%	33%	5%
% car ownership	98%	64%	39%
Average number of rooms	6.9	5.9	4.8
Average number of other persons in home	.1	.4	.3
% having major health problems	9%	16%	13%
% members of library (any family member)	35%	25%	10%
% having dictionary in home	91%	65%	24%
% having magazine(s) in home	86%	51%	43%
% who had visited a museum	42%	20%	2%
% who had visited a zoo	72%	49%	26%

[1] Wave 0 and 1 only, experimental and control groups combined

[2] Occupation Ratings: 1 = unskilled; 2 = semi-skilled; 3 = skilled; 4 = professional

better the performance of children on this test, the more likely they are to succeed in schools based on traditional academic models). The score range of 50 to 85 was selected for a very practical reason: special-education funds were available from the state to aid children certified "educable mentally retarded" based on demonstrated performance within that range in the absence of discernible organic impairments.

Sampling procedures

During September of each project year, Perry School census data were used to locate all families in the attendance area who had three-year-old children (four-year-old children in the case of Wave 0). These families were then interviewed to obtain information for computing SES ratings. Next, children of those families rated at or below 11 points on the SES index were administered Stanford-Binet Intelligence Scales. Finally, children scoring between 50 and 85 on the Binet[2] and judged to evidence no organic impairment by the examining psychologist became part of the sampling universe. As it happened, virtually all eligible children were enrolled in the project during its five years of operation, approximately 25% of the total preschool-age population at that time within the attendance area.

Assignment to treatment groups

Research staff went to considerable lengths to ensure the comparability of treatment groups within each wave. Experimental and control groups were not pre-existing groups, nor were they formed by self-selection. Consequently, the existence of motivational differences between parents in the two groups with regard to obtaining preschool education for their children seems extremely unlikely. Moreover, teachers and others who might have had vested interests in the particular composition of classrooms and firsthand knowledge of eligible families were excluded from the assignment process. In practice, the following procedures were used to assign eligible families to one of two treatment conditions. First, all children were rank-ordered according to Stanford-Binet scores. Next, they were sorted (odd/even) into two groups. If these groups had unequal sex ratios or unequal SES ratings, they were equated by exchanging children, with Stanford-Binet scores held more or less constant. Groups roughly equated in this manner were assigned to treatment conditions by a "flip of the coin".

Following the assignment of Waves 0 and 1 in 1962, these procedures had to be qualified somewhat by practical considerations. In order to restrict the diffusion effects to treatment within families, younger siblings of children already in the project were assigned to the same group, such

---

[2]Occasionally children were enrolled even though they scored slightly above the prescribed ceiling of 85. In some instances, this was done in order to fill preschool vacancies in the experimental group and then to balance the control group; in other instances, to include sibs of children already in the project. Eight children in the experimental group and 11 children in the control group had initial IQ scores ranging from 86 through 88.

that assignment was by family rather than child. Eligible children who remained after the forced assignment of siblings were then allocated to treatment conditions in the manner described above. Occasional exchanges of children between groups also had to be made because of the inconvenience of half-day preschool for working mothers and the transportation difficulties of some families. No funds were available for transportation or full day care, and special arrangements could not always be made.

Although pure, true randomization was not achieved, the outcome of these assignment procedures was such that it seems legitimate, for purposes of statistical analysis, to treat the experimental and control groups as independent samples drawn from the same population. When experimental and control children were compared on the three assignment criteria—initial Stanford-Binet score, SES, and sex—no differences appeared (Table 4). Linear discriminant analysis comparing the two treatment groups on these three criteria simultaneously also failed to differentiate them (D = .038; F = .385; p = .76). In short, there is no apparent reason to believe that post-treatment differences can be explained by pre-treatment differences on motivational factors or assignment criteria.

Two other factors, however, might confound experimental results, working to the advantage of control-group children. First, "horizontal

Table 4

*Comparison of Treatment Groups on
Assignment Criteria*

Initial IQ

GROUP	N	MEAN	S.D.
Experimental	58	79.6	5.9
Control	65	78.5	6.9

F Ratio: <1; N.S.

SES

GROUP	N	MEAN	S.D.
Experimental	58	8.44	1.24
Control	65	8.30	1.12

F Ratio: <1; N.S.

Sex Distribution

	MALE	FEMALE	
Experimental	33	25	58
Control	39	26	65
	72	51	123

$x^2 = .122$; N.S.

18

diffusion" of treatment effects has been observed to operate within socially bounded subpopulations in urban areas (Gray and Klaus, 1969), with the result that control-group children benefit in some degree from the preschool treatment intended for children in the experimental group. It seems likely that horizontal diffusion occurred within the Perry School attendance area at some level. Unfortunately, it is not possible to test this hypothesis or to control for such effects within the experimental design described here. Second, there is some suggestion in data collected with the Perry Demographic Questionnaire that control-group families may be more upwardly mobile than families in the experimental group and that this may have positively affected their children's later performance. The only significant difference between treatment groups on initial demographic-SES measures was in mother's employment (Table 5): there were more working mothers in the control (31%) than in the experimental group (9%) (chi-square = 9.28; p<.01). This difference was not explained by differences in father absence, family size, or other variables on which data were collected. (The problem of enrolling children of working mothers in the half-day preschool program has already been discussed.)

Whether the employment status of mothers at project enrollment predicts later socio-economic mobility remains to be determined on the basis of data now being collected as part of the continuing longitudinal study. Of more immediate concern, however, is the possibility that the academic achievement of children of working mothers is different from the achievement of other children, systematically biasing comparisons in favor of one group or the other. A careful examination of the relationships between mother's employment status (1 = not working; 2+ = working) at project entry and child outcomes indicated that when mother's employment status was correlated with child outcomes, it was positively correlated—i.e., the children of working mothers scored higher than other children. Thus, initial differences in the distribution of working mothers across groups worked to the advantage of control-group children, inflating their scores on some measures at some time-points. No systematic attempt was made in the analyses reported here to adjust treatment-group means by covarying on mother's employment status. In analysis of California Achievement Test performance and School Success during the post-treatment period, however, the influence of mother's employment status upon child outcomes will be briefly examined because of evidence that treatment-group differences on these outcomes were significantly attenuated by initial group differences in the distribution of working mothers.

General demographic characteristics of the treatment groups

Information presented in Tables 5 and 6 was extracted from the Perry Demographic Questionnaire, which was administered to each family prior to project enrollment.[3] Data were tabulated for each child, disregard-

---

[3]Slight discrepancies in the descriptive statistics presented in this and the previous report are the result of corrections made in original data files.

Table 5

General Demographic Characteristics:
Treatment Groups and Total Sample

VARIABLES	EXPERIMENTAL GROUP (N=58)			CONTROL GROUP (N=65)			GROUP MAIN EFFECT	TOTAL SAMPLE (N=123)		
	(N)	MEAN	(S.D.)	(N)	MEAN	(S.D.)	F RATIO[3]	(N)	MEAN	(S.D.)
Child's Age at Entry (months)[1]	(58)	42.7	(6.2)	(65)	41.9	(5.9)	2.68	(123)	42.3	(6.0)
Father's Age	(28)	31.5	(5.0)	(31)	34.0	(8.2)	<1	(59)	32.8	(6.9)
Mother's Age	(57)	29.6	(6.2)	(62)	28.7	(6.9)	<1	(119)	29.1	(6.6)
Number of Children in Family	(58)	4.9	(2.4)	(65)	4.9	(2.7)	2.55	(123)	4.9	(2.6)
Number of Younger Siblings	(58)	1.0	(0.1)	(65)	1.0	(0.1)	<1	(123)	1.0	(0.1)
Number of Older Siblings	(58)	2.8	(1.3)	(65)	3.0	(1.8)	<1	(123)	2.9	(1.6)
SES Rating	(58)	8.4	(1.2)	(65)	8.3	(1.1)	<1	(123)	8.4	(1.2)
Father's Education	(38)	8.4	(2.3)	(34)	8.8	(2.5)	<1	(72)	8.6	(2.4)
Mother's Education	(58)	9.5	(2.4)	(65)	9.4	(2.0)	<1	(123)	9.4	(2.2)
Father's Employment Level[2]	(33)	2.2	(0.8)	(33)	2.0	(0.6)	<1	(66)	2.1	(0.7)
Mother's Employment Level[2]	(58)	1.1	(0.3)	(65)	1.3	(0.5)	6.75**	(123)	1.2	(0.4)
Head of Household's Employment Level[2]	(58)	1.7	(0.8)	(65)	1.7	(0.6)	<1	(123)	1.7	(0.7)
Number of Rooms in Home	(58)	5.2	(1.2)	(65)	5.2	(1.6)	<1	(123)	5.2	(1.4)
Density in Home (Rooms/Persons)	(58)	0.9	(0.3)	(65)	0.8	(0.3)	<1	(123)	0.9	(0.3)

[1]The mean entry age is inflated to 3½ years by the inclusion of Wave 0 children, who entered the project at 4½ years of age. The average age of children in Waves 1-4 was 3⅓ years.

[2]Code for employment levels: 0 = No data (appears only for fathers in father absent homes)
    1 = Unemployed
    2 = Unskilled Employment
    3 = Semiskilled Employment
    4 = Skilled Employment (including lower managerial)
    5 = Professional Employment (no cases in sample)

[3]The F ratio reported here was obtained from a three-way analysis of variance: group by sex by wave.

Asterisks indicate significance level (*$p<.10$; **$p<.05$; ***$p<.01$). If no asterisks appear, the difference is not significant at or beyond the .10 level.

Table 6

General Demographic Characteristics:
Treatment Groups (with Chi-Square Tests on Distributions) and Total Sample

VARIABLES	EXPERIMENTAL GROUP (N=58)		CONTROL GROUP (N=65)		X^2	TOTAL SAMPLE (N=123)	
	N	%	N	%		N	%
Father Present	32	55%	33	51%	< 1	65	53%
Father Absent	26	45%	32	49%		58	47%
Nuclear Family Household	8	14%	13	20%		21	17%
Extended Household	47	81%	52	80%	< 1[a]	99	80%
Unknown	3	4%	0	0%		3	3%
Mother Born in South	40	69%	45	69%		85	69%
Mother Born Elsewhere	8	14%	15	23%	1.10[a]	23	19%
Unknown	10	17%	5	8%		15	12%
Population of Mother's Birthplace:							
Under 9,999	16	28%	22	34%		38	31%
10,000-99,999	14	24%	24	37%		38	31%
100,000-499,999	10	17%	8	12%	1.81[a]	18	15%
500,000 +	2	3%	2	3%		4	3%
Unknown	16	28%	9	14%		25	20%
Family on Welfare	33	57%	29	45%		62	50%
Family not on Welfare	24	41%	35	54%	1.91[a]	59	48%
Unknown	1	2%	1	2%		2	2%
Religion:							
Baptist	36	62%	41	63%		77	63%
Other Protestant	8	14%	12	19%		20	16%
Catholic	0	0%	2	3%	2.05[a]	2	2%
No Church	1	2%	2	3%		3	2%
Unknown	13	22%	8	12%		21	17%
Employment of Parents:							
Both Employed	5	9%	7	11%		12	10%
Father Alone Employed	23	39%	22	34%	9.71*	45	37%
Mother Alone Employed	2	4%	14	22%		16	13%
Neither Employed	28	48%	22	34%		50	41%

[a]All categories were used to calculate marginals and expected cell frequencies. Although "unknown" categories were excluded from computations of chi-square, the obtained chi-square was tested using the degrees of freedom associated with the contingency table based on all categories.

Asterisks indicate significance level (*p<.10; **p<.05; ***p<.01). If no asterisks appear, the difference is not significant at or beyond the .10 level.

ing family membership. Consequently, some families are, in a sense, over-represented since more than one child may have been enrolled in the project.[4] With the exception of mother's employment, the two treatment groups were very similar.

Sample attrition

Sample attrition has been slight. Three children in the experimental group moved before completing preschool; one child in the control group moved shortly after enrollment; and one child died. These losses reduced the original sample from 128 children to the 123 children who constitute the "total sample" of this longitudinal study. In no year following pre-school have fewer than 90% of all children been located and tested. While nine children were either not found or, for some other reason, not tested in fourth grade, all were subsequently located as of that grade in a search of school records for grade retention and special-education data. In 1973, 84% of project families still lived in Ypsilanti, and only one child (control group) out of 123 could not be found.

Independent variables

Preschool: the experimental treatment

Although the preschool program was not systematically documented over the course of the project, the reader can gain a good sense of curriculum evolution from *Preschool Intervention: A Preliminary Report of the Perry Preschool Project* (Weikart, 1967) and of the resultant curriculum model from *The Cognitively Oriented Curriculum: A Framework for Preschool Teachers* (Weikart, Rogers, Adcock, and McClelland, 1971).[5] A brief over-view of the preschool program will be presented here.

Children in the experimental group attended preschool for half-days, five days a week from mid-October through May. Each year about 12 three-year-olds and the same number of four-year-olds were enrolled, sharing the same classroom and teachers. The staff/child ratio was ap-proximately 1:6 for all waves. During the preschool year, experimental-group children and their mothers in all waves were visited every week in their homes by preschool teachers. The primary objective of these visits,

---

[4]In the experimental group there were six pairs of siblings, one group of three siblings, and one group of four siblings. Thus, the 58 children in the experimental group were members of 47 families. In the control group, there were 12 pairs of siblings, and the 65 children were members of 53 families.

[5]The preschool curriculum has undergone further development in subsequent projects. A more recent curriculum statement can be found in a publication available through the High/Scope Educational Research Foundation: *Young Children in Action—A Manual for Preschool Educators*, by Mary Hohmann and Bernard Banet, with a Foreword by David P. Weikart, 1978. Films produced to support training in the curriculum are described in the High/Scope catalog of audio-visual materials, available from the Foundation on request.

which lasted about 90 minutes, was to involve each mother in the education of her child.

From the beginning, the preschool program was explicitly concerned with supporting the development of the child's cognitive skills through individualized teaching-learning. Although this objective was maintained, the curriculum model and its implementation developed substantially from 1962 through 1967. The Ypsilanti Perry Preschool Project did not represent a prefabricated solution to preschool education. It was a major developmental effort which drew upon a broad spectrum of research in child development and early childhood education and, perhaps more importantly, upon the concrete experiences of its own staff to formulate a coherent and effective program. Summary descriptions of the program for each school year follow:

- 1962-63 (Wave 0 and Wave 1): Although lesson plans provided a modicum of structure, the program had no systematic theory base and only loosely articulated objectives. On the other hand, there was tremendous enthusiasm among teachers and a great deal of thoughtful experimentation—both crucial ingredients of success.

- 1963-64 (Wave 1 and Wave 2): A transitional year. Goals became better articulated and teaching more individualized as teachers learned more about the specific developmental problems, needs, and interests of preschool-age children. Six seminars were held for staff on Piagetian theory.

- 1964-65 (Wave 2 and Wave 3): Systematic daily planning and evaluation by teachers, emphasizing the needs and interests of individual children, became an integral part of the program and provided explicit structure. Although curriculum development gained impetus and direction from the work of Jean Piaget, the program was not yet systematically theory-based.

- 1965-66 (Wave 3 and Wave 4): Formalizing patterns that had emerged during the preceding year, the preschool day was organized into a sequence of activity periods: planning time; work time; group meeting for evaluation; cleanup; juice and group time; activity time; circle time; and dismissal (Weikart, Rogers, Adcock, and McClelland, 1971). Teachers' understanding of developmental needs and processes among the children were increasingly derived from Piagetian theory, and they made systematic attempts to evaluate the appropriateness of their own classroom behavior with reference to this theory.

- 1966-67 (Wave 4 and Wave 5[6]): The largely Piagetian theory base of the curriculum was consolidated and a coherent, explicit model formulated.

The preschool experience of each wave was in some degree different from that of other waves due to changes in the treatment variable over the course of the project. Thus, neither all five waves nor any subset thereof represents a set of exact, "formal" replications. However, since the experimental treatment was not systematically manipulated and since there

---

[6]Wave 5 became part of the "pilot wave" of the subsequent Curriculum Demonstration Project (Weikart et al., 1970). These children served as "junior preschoolers" to Wave 4 in the final year of the Ypsilanti Perry Preschool Project.

was no consistent pattern of effects differentiating waves, it was decided to treat all waves as "practical" replications of the experiment for purposes of the longitudinal study.[7]

Following completion of preschool for the experimental group each year, both experimental and control children entered regular public-school kindergarten (most at the Perry School in Ypsilanti, Michigan) just as they would have done had there been no intervention. No effort was made to assign children to particular teachers, and no effort was made to alter the elementary-school curriculum in any way. In short, after the completion of preschool, absolutely no further intervention occurred, other than annual testing of both experimental and control children. Elementary teachers were not informed whether children had been in the experimental or control group, and few teachers had any knowledge of the aims and procedures of the experimental preschool. (Kindergarten teachers, however, were often able to identify experimental children by their classroom comments about preschool experiences.) Although post-kindergarten school environments have become increasingly diverse for project children, there is no evidence that children from one group have attended schools that are in any sense "better" or "worse" than those attended by children in the other group.

Sex of child

The previous report of longitudinal results from the Perry Preschool Project (Weikart, Deloria, Lawser, and Wiegerink, 1970) noted differences in the effects of preschool on boys and girls. Other studies (e.g., Beller, 1969) have reported similar findings. In order to address the general issue of sex differences and in particular to evaluate our earlier findings using complete data on all waves through fourth grade, sex of child has been included as an independent factor in all analysis-of-variance designs employed in this study.

Initial child measures[8]

Four standardized tests of academic potential were administered to children at FEY:

- Stanford-Binet Intelligence Scale (Binet: Terman and Merrill, 1960)
- Peabody Picture Vocabulary Test (PPVT: Dunn, 1965)
- Illinois Test of Psycholinguistic Abilities, Experimental Edition (ITPA: McCarthy and Kirk, 1961)
- Arthur Adaptation of the Leiter International Performance Scale (Leiter: Arthur, 1952)

---

[7]What differences did emerge across waves seem more likely the result of sampling error than of differences in preschool experience, given the small number of children in each Wave and the overall similarity of outcomes. Wave is incorporated as a "blocking factor" (cf., Myers, 1972, p. 152ff.) in the analysis of variance designs utilized in this study to increase their efficiency. The main effects of wave and of the interactions of wave with other independent factors are reported in analysis of variance tables so that the reader can evaluate the decisions discussed here.

[8]These instruments are discussed in greater detail in appendix A.

Of these tests only the Binet was a true premeasure, the others having been administered up to three months after children entered the project (Table 7).

In order to include the FEY PPVT, FEY ITPA, and FEY Leiter as independent variables in regression analyses predicting child outcomes, the variance in these measures associated with treatment-group membership was removed. More specifically, these variables were regressed on the dichotomous treatment variable (experimental/control) producing residual scores: FEY PPVT/R, FEY ITPA/R, and FEY Leiter/R. These variables were combined with FEY Binet to form an independent (predictor) variable set—*Entering Child Characteristics*—that was incorporated in regression analyses exploring the relative contributions of experimental and pre-experimental factors to child outcomes.[9]

Home background variables

Information about the home environment of each child was collected using three instruments:[10]

- *PDQ*: Perry Demographic Questionnaire (project staff)
- *CHES*: Cognitive Home Environment Scale (adapted by project staff from Wolf, 1964)
- *MAI*: Maternal Attitude Inventory (adapted by project staff from Schaefer and Bell, 1958)

Demographic-SES data from the PDQ were obtained prior to project enrollment and were clearly not affected by the experimental treatment. The MAI was administered twice to mothers of children in each wave: once shortly after entering the project (FEY) and again after an interval of about six months (SEY). The entering fall scores (post-FEY) were used to form a measure of maternal childrearing attitudes, independent of treatment, by removing that part of the variance in these scores which was associated with treatment.[11] These "residual" MAI scores and various demographic-SES variables appear in multiple regression analyses as independent variables predicting children's performance on measures of academic potential and their actual success in school.

The CHES was developed after the project was well underway and was administered during a single calendar year (1966) to families in all waves. The youngest children (Wave 4) were just finishing their first year of preschool (SEY), while the oldest (Wave 0) were already in second

---

[9]Regression analysis designs are described more fully in appendix B.

[10]Data from all of these instruments were analyzed in the 1970 Perry Report. Two of the three instruments have undergone further development since that time: Maternal Attitude Inventory (formerly called the Inventory of Attitudes of Family Life and Children) and the Cognitive Home Environment Scale.

[11]MAI scores were regressed on the dichotomous treatment variable (experimental/control), and the differences between actual and predicted scores (residuals) became the new MAI variable: MAI/R. The net effect of these procedures was to equate group means. Less than 3% of the variance in MAI scores was explained by treatment-group membership.

grade (see Table 1). This pattern of data collection was inconsistent with the basic longitudinal design and seriously complicates the interpretation of CHES data. It is quite possible that certain interactional and attitudinal factors assessed by the CHES are related to age of child, and thus to wave. Also, certain CHES variables might have been affected by the home-visit component of the experimental treatment, making CHES variables dependent rather than independent factors. Before analyzing the CHES, certain items on which maternal response varied systematically with age of child were eliminated. Two independent scales were then derived by factor analyzing the remaining CHES items. Finally, those portions of the variance in CHES scores associated with treatment and wave were removed. The resulting "residual" CHES scores were included as independent variables in multiple regression analyses along with other environmental measures.[12] Although this solution was not ideal, it seemed to represent a reasonable alternative to dismissing these potentially important data entirely.

Five home-background variables—Mother's Education, SES, FEY MAI/R, CHES1/R, and CHES2/R—are incorporated in regression analyses as an independent variable set predicting child outcomes. As a group these variables are called *Home Environment Factors*.

Dependent variables

Dependent variables in the experimental design can be assigned to four broad categories of measurement: academic aptitude and achievement, social-emotional development, home environment, and school success. Each will be considered in turn. Table 7 presents a complete listing of instruments referred to in this volume and information about their administration.

Academic aptitude and achievement

Indicators of academic aptitude and achievement include the following instruments:

- *Binet*: Stanford-Binet Intelligence Scale, Form L-M, 1937 Revision (Terman and Merrill, 1960)
- *ITPA*: Illinois Test of Psycholinguistic Abilities, Experimental Version (McCarthy and Kirk, 1961 and 1963)
- *PPVT*: Peabody Picture Vocabulary Test (Dunn, 1965)
- *Leiter*: Arthur Adaptation of the Leiter International Performance Scale (Arthur, 1952)

---

[12]CHES scores were regressed on the dichotomous treatment variable (experimental/control) and on the categorical wave variable coded as four dummy variables (Cohen, 1968). The differences between actual and predicted scores (residuals) became the new CHES variables: CHES1/R and CHS2/R. Less than 2% of the variance in CHES1 scores and less than 3% of the variance of CHES2 scores were explained by treatment group and wave.

Table 7

Instruments and Their Administration

INSTRUMENT	TO WHOM ADMINISTERED	BY WHOM ADMINISTERED	WAVES ON WHICH DATA WERE COLLECTED AT EACH TESTPOINT								
			FEY PRE[1]	FEY POST[2]	SEY	S2Y[3]	SKG	S1G	S2G	S3G	S4G
Stanford-Binet Intelligence Scale (Binet)	Children	Certified Testers	0-4	—	0-4	1-4	0-4	0-4	0-4	0-4	0-4
Peabody Picture Vocabulary Test (PPVT)	Children	Certified Testers	—	0-4	2-4	1-4	0-4	0-4	0-4	0-4	—
Arthur Adaptation of the Leiter International Performance Scale (Leiter)	Children	Certified Testers	—	0-4	2-4	1-4	0-4	0-4	0-4	0-4	—
Illinois Test of Psycholinguistic Abilities (ITPA)	Children	Certified Testers	—	0-4	—	1-4	0-4	0-4	0-4	0-4	—
California Achievement Test, Lower and Upper Primary (CAT)	Children	Trained Testers	—	—	—	—	—	0-4	0-4	0-4	0,2-4
Ypsilanti Rating Scale (YRS)	Teachers	Self-Administered	—	—	—	—	0-4	0-4	0-2,4	0-4	—
Pupil Behavior Inventory (PBI)	Teachers	Self-Administered	—	—	—	—	0-4	0-4	0-2,4	0-3	—
Maternal Attitude Inventory (MAI)	Mothers	Preschool Teachers (trained)	—	0-4	0-3	—	—	—	—	—	—
Cognitive Home Environment Scale (CHES)	Mothers	Preschool Teachers & Research Assistants	—	—	—	4	3	2	1	0	—
Perry Demographic Questionnaire (PDQ)	Parents	Preschool Teachers	0-4	—	—	—	—	—	—	—	—

[1]"FEY PRE": just prior to project enrollment

[2]"FEY POST": 0-3 months after project enrollment

[3]Wave 0 received only one year of preschool; its spring data are listed with SEY data from the other waves.

- *CAT:* California Achievement Test, Lower and Upper Primary Forms (Tiegs and Clark, 1957a and 1957b)
- *PBI:* Pupil Behavior Inventory, Academic Motivation Scale (Vinter, Sarri, Vorwaller, and Schafer, 1966)
- *YRS:* Ypsilanti Rating Scale, Academic Potential and Verbal Skill Scales (project staff)

The YRS and PBI are teacher rating scales; descriptions are provided in appendix A. Issues of concurrent and predictive validity and of reliability specific to the project sample are also considered in appendix A. The discussion here will focus on more general questions of validity of the major standardized tests: Binet, ITPA, PPVT, Leiter, and CAT.

In this study, standardized test scores are assumed to indicate academic potential, or to predict school success, rather than measure psychological traits such as "intelligence" or "learning capacity". Although this position does not seem to be open to most of the criticism that has been leveled against the use of standardized tests in educational evaluation, a brief discussion of the controversy may help to place the research reported here in better perspective.

Educational evaluation tends to rely heavily upon standardized tests of cognitive, linguistic, and academic skills development. Whether the problem is to diagnose individual learning difficulties or "deficiencies", to decide who is most "gifted", to rank schools according to "academic quality", or to assess the effectiveness of particular teachers or curricula in achieving educational objectives, the most widely accepted solution is to test the child. This mode of evaluation has been particularly prominent in research concerned with early childhood education for low-income and minority-group children. In these studies, preschool program success has been evaluated largely on the basis of whether children's scores on standardized tests of aptitude have been brought closer to population, or more often white middle-class, norms.

Performance differentials either between groups or within groups over time, however, can be difficult to interpret. Whether or not higher levels of performance on the Binet, ITPA, PPVT, Leiter, or CAT indicate that children "think" or "learn" better depends upon the degree to which the implied constructs actually account for the variances in test scores. Such an interpretation, however, would be invalidated by evidence that something other than the psychological traits of "intelligence" and "learning capacity" explains the observed performance differentials separating low-income and minority-group children from their white middle-class peers. A number of alternative explanations merit serious attention.

It may be that the typically poor performance of so-called "disadvantaged" children on standardized tests is the result of class and cultural differences between these children and those in the standardization populations.[13] Thus, performance gains associated with preschool attendance

---

[13]Of the five tests considered here—Binet, PPVT, ITPA, Leiter, and CAT—only CAT norms were based on a sample including nonwhite subjects; only CAT and Binet standardization samples were drawn from all geographical regions in the United States; and only the CAT standardization sample seems likely on the basis of information made available by the authors, to have adequately represented all SES levels in the populations. Even when

would indicate, not higher levels of cognitive or communicative functioning, but a higher degree of assimilation into mainstream culture. The research of Edward Zigler and colleagues (Zigler and Butterfield, 1968; Zigler, Abelson, and Seitz, 1973) challenges claims that preschool programs evidencing performance gains on standardized tests have actually altered the formal cognitive or linguistic processes of participating children. They argue instead that both the differences between economically disadvantaged and nondisadvantaged children *and* the frequent preschool-associated gains of the former are substantially, if not entirely, explained by a pronounced "wariness of the test situation" and an "outer-directed problem-solving style" among economically disadvantaged children which are attenuated by the preschool experience.

Perhaps more widely recognized is the ethnocentricity of specific content and prescribed "right" answers in commonly used standardized tests (see, e.g., Jorgensen, 1973; Waddel and Cahoon, 1970). Since no attempt was made to sample subcultural domains in developing the tests considered here, substantial portions of test content may be unfamiliar to children who do not share the specific life experiences of their white and/or middle-class peers. Consequently, it is likely that the poor performance of low-income and minority-group children results at least in part from their unfamiliarity with test content and that performance gains associated with preschool are related to increased familiarity.

Without exhausting the possibilities, another alternative hypothesis should be mentioned: that middle-class children, but not lower-class children, acquire picture- and word-association patterns (as conditioned responses) which permit them to "correctly" answer certain test questions even though they are incapable of logically deriving the right answer, given their level (defined by Piagetian theory) of cognitive development (Meier, 1973). The lower-class child in this situation must rely upon his own ingenuity, with no guarantee that an answer which is entirely appropriate to his level of cognitive development is what the adult test-makers consider correct. Again, preschool programs may simply "condition" the child to respond in test-appropriate ways without altering underlying cognitive processes. In the face of such uncertainty, to claim that "intelligence is what intelligence tests measure" is not enough. It is meaningless to use standardized test scores as evaluational criteria unless there is some consensus, or at least a presumption by the researcher, as to what is being measured.

In the longitudinal study, then, it has been assumed that the Binet, ITPA, PPVT, Leiter, and CAT measure certain skills, learned or otherwise, which have been (and remain) important in prevailing academic environments. Specifically, it was hypothesized that children who perform well on these tests would have an advantage over children who perform poorly, so far as traditional academic tasks are concerned. This hypothesis was particularly reasonable since, whatever they purport to measure, all of these tests were explicitly designed to predict academic performance in school and/or to diagnose educational-learning disabilities for purposes

---

standardization samples are representative of the population at large, however, test norms are primarily determined by the performance of white, nonpoor children, who numerically dominate the school-age population.

of remediation. The actual relationships between test performance and academic success among children in this sample will be explored in the section "Findings for the post-treatment period" in chapter II.

Measures of social-emotional development

Two instruments were employed to assess the social and emotional development of children:

- *YRS:* Ypsilanti Rating Scale—Social Development and Emotional Adjustment Factors (project staff)

- *PBI:* Pupil Behavior Inventory—Socio-Emotional State, Classroom Conduct, Teacher Dependence, and Personal Behavior Scales (Vinter, Sarri, Vorwaller, and Schafer, 1966)

Both instruments are rating scales on which each child was rated by his teachers in kindergarten, first, second, and third grades. This measurement approach was designed to provide a picture of children's behavior as teachers, not clinical psychologists, view it. No presumption was made that social maturity and appropriateness of behavior as judged by teachers represents the only legitimate way of viewing social-emotional development in children. However, the opinion of teachers is crucial to school success, and the ability to behave appropriately, in this sense, was considered to be a possible practical benefit of preschool. More detailed consideration of the YRS and PBI is given in appendix A.

Home environment

It was anticipated that the home-teaching component of the experimental treatment might alter certain dimensions of the home environments of children who attended preschool. Two instruments were used to obtain information about the home environments of all children in the sample:[14]

- *CHES:* Cognitive Home Environment Scale (adapted by project staff from Wolf, 1964)

- *MAI:* Maternal Attitude Inventory (adapted by project staff from Schaefer and Bell, 1958)

The CHES scales were designed to measure the extent to which home environments were supportive of cognitive development and the formal educational process. The MAI was intended to assess the similarity of maternal childrearing attitudes to local middle-class norms. Both CHES and MAI data were obtained by interviewing mothers. Specific issues of instrument construction and of validity and reliability are taken up in appendix A.

---

[14]The problem of determining the "dependent" or "independent" status of CHES and MAI variables in the experimental design is addressed in appendix A.

School success

Although measurement of child outcomes through fourth grade focused on "indices" of academic aptitude and achievement, a more important question was how well children were actually doing in school. Stated somewhat differently, if experimental-group children were not more successful in school than children from the control group, the preschool program could not be considered effective in terms of its own goals, no matter how beneficial the program may have been in other respects.

On the basis of a preliminary study conducted within the Ypsilanti public schools (see the 1970 Perry Report), children living in what became the project area were identified as those least likely to succeed in school. Moreover, the project enrolled only the highest risk children from this area: those whose families were at the lowest SES levels and who met (on the basis of one test at three years of age) State of Michigan criteria for special education certification as "educable mentally retarded" (see "Sample" section above). Consequently, the original academic prognosis for project children was bleak: that many, if not most, would fail in school, i.e., be retained in grade and/or placed in special education programs. The measure of school success employed in this study was selected specifically to evaluate this prognosis.

Data were obtained from the public schools classifying each child into one of three categories for each of four years following kindergarten: on grade, regular classroom; retained in grade, regular classroom; or placed in special education program. Children who were on grade and in regular classrooms were considered "successful"; other children were deemed "unsuccessful". Although this criterion would not be particularly useful for evaluating school achievement among children in general, it seemed to be the most appropriate measure for the project sample.[15] Moreover, differential rates of retention and special education placement across treatment groups would represent different costs to the educational system and have direct implications for economic policy decisions regarding the allocation of limited resources to preschool programs.

There are, of course, legitimate questions as to whether success in contemporary public school environments ought to be the ultimate evaluational criterion of preschool programs. David McClelland (1973), for example, has argued that while performance on aptitude tests may predict performance in school, neither does a very good job of predicting success in life. Jencks et al. (1972) have developed this thesis further. And research by Jane Mercer (1971) suggests that the categorization of minority-group children as "educable mentally retarded" by public schools is frequently unjustified, since these children function quite adequately in their own social-cultural spheres. In the continuing longitudinal study of sample children, attempts are being made to assess nonacademic competencies in order to provide a broader developmental view.

---

[15]Grades were not used for several reasons: (1) pupil evaluation schemes varied from one school district to another and within the same district from year to year (in some districts grades as such are no longer given to elementary-school children); (2) school personnel raised serious questions about the comparability of grades given by different teachers within the same school and, particularly, across schools; (3) children placed in special education programs would have to be excluded from the sample in any group comparisons using grades; (4) grades have no clear cost implication.

Data collection

General procedures

Data collection procedures are outlined in Table 7 for each instrument considered in this report. The discussion here will be limited to a consideration of the conditions of standardized test administration during treatment and post-treatment periods.

Annual testing was performed by qualified testers who had completed formal training in the administration of individual intelligence tests. As a precautionary measure, research staff reviewed each test, item by item, with every examiner. In addition, efforts were made to impress testers with the importance of establishing good rapport with each child and of optimizing the environmental conditions of the test in order to obtain maximum levels of performance. If children seemed to give up too easily, testers were instructed to reassure them and encourage them to keep trying until it was apparent that they had performed as well as they could under the circumstances. Children who were untestable on a scheduled day, for whatever reason, were rescheduled for testing at a later time whenever possible. The Stanford-Binet, ITPA, PPVT, and Leiter were administered individually in two sessions, the Binet and PPVT usually being administered in one session and the Leiter and ITPA in the other. California Achievement Tests were administered to small groups of children (six or less). To minimize the possible confounding effects of tester differences, children from the experimental and control groups from different waves and of both sexes were assigned to each tester in as balanced a manner as possible within ever-present scheduling constraints.

Preschool years

During the preschool years, testing was not "blind". That is, the examiners who administered standardized tests (Binet, PPVT, ITPA, and Leiter) knew which children were attending preschool and which were not. Furthermore, they were usually aware of the purposes of the experiment. Although testers employed in the project were highly professional, it is conceivable that the *measured* performance of children during the preschool period was biased positively in favor of the experimental group and/or negatively against the control group. Of course, since evaluation of the experimental treatment hinges ultimately upon subsequent rather than concurrent effects, the possibility of biases in preschool data does not call into question the longitudinal findings.

Post-treatment period

Once children entered school, testing became "blind", with occasional child-initiated exceptions in early grades. Moreover, post-treatment testers had little if any knowledge of the purposes of the experiment. Consequently, even if testers discovered to which group a child belonged on the basis of comments made during the test situation, they had no vested interest in the results of the test.

Data processing

Preparation of data

Techniques for the transfer and transformation of raw data into more manageable forms have changed somewhat in response to changes in computer technology. The formal process, however, has remained the same. The following steps have been followed by data processing staff in preparing project data for statistical analysis: verification of any computations (e.g., test scores) already on protocols; preliminary coding-scoring of raw data, when necessary; verification of the preceding step; transfer of codes and/or scores onto some information storage device compatible with available computers (punch-cards or, more recently, magnetic discs and tapes via remote terminals); verification of transferred data against original sources.

In preparation for the analyses reported here, a highly accessible and flexible longitudinal data structure was created utilizing the Michigan Interactive Data Analysis System (MIDAS) developed by the Statistical Research Laboratory of the University of Michigan, Ann Arbor (Fox and Guire, 1973). All variables considered in this report were incorporated. The distributions of scores on each variable were closely examined to identify possible erroneous entries, and all suspiciously high and low scores and those falling outside the possible range were verified against raw data on the original protocols. Additional checks were made on the internal consistency of data.

Computer facilities and programs

All statistical calculations were performed on the University of Michigan Computing Center's IBM/360 model 67 dual processor computer. The computer programs used in analyzing data for this report were drawn from a number of sources. Descriptive statistics were obtained using programs available in MIDAS. The MIDAS system was also used in computing correlations (programs: MCORREL and CORREL), analyzing contingency tables (program: TWOWAY), performing multiple linear discriminant analyses (program: DISCRIMINANT), and performing principal component factor analyses and Varimax rotations of the principal axes (programs: FACTOR and ROTATE). Conventional three-way analyses of variance were computed using program AVAR23 adapted from Veldman (1967). Finally, multiple linear regression analyses were performed using program LINEAR (Kelly, Beggs, McNeil, Eichelberger, and Lyon, 1969).

II Research findings

Overview

Prior to this volume, the most complete presentation of Perry Preschool Project findings appeared in the 1970 Perry Report (Weikart, Deloria, Lawser, and Wiegerink, 1970), which analyzed data collected from initiation of the project with Waves 0 and 1 in 1962 through the graduation of Wave 4 from preschool in the spring of 1967.[16] However, results presented in the previous report were definitive only with respect to the preschool period; all longitudinal findings reported for the early elementary grades were preliminary and tentative.

In this chapter, data on the total sample from project enrollment (FEY) through fourth grade (S4G) are analyzed. The central issue of preschool effectiveness is addressed from a somewhat broader perspective than in the previous report, utilizing recently collected data on actual school success, i.e., grade and class placement. The sections of this chapter present and discuss findings from the preschool and post-treatment periods, respectively. Extensive description and analysis of the measures used may be found in appendix A; the statistical methodology applied is described in appendix B. The reader may wish to review these appendices before reading further in this chapter. Supplemental descriptive statistics (for treatment groups, waves, boys and girls), bivariate correlations (between all variables within each treatment group), and specifications of all models used in regression analysis appear in the separately published *Statistical Supplement* to this report.

Research questions

Before proceeding with the presentation of findings from this study, it is important to articulate the specific questions guiding the research. The initial statement of research questions will be quite general. Subsequently, these questions will be restated as testable questions and hypotheses in terms of specific analytic designs.

The central question in this study is whether children who attended preschool benefited from that experience. The basic research strategy for answering this question was comparison of the experimental (preschool) group with a control (no preschool) group, rather than assessment of change within the experimental group. The findings presented in this volume address six basic questions involving comparisons of experimental and control children:

1. Did experimental-group children who attended preschool (a) score higher on standardized measures of aptitude and achievement, (b) appear more socially and emotionally mature to elementary-school

---

[16]The replication factors within the experimental design are discussed at length under "Replication" in chapter I. Tables 1 and 2 illustrate the stepwise progression of waves through preschool and elementary grades and clearly define the data base of the 1970 Perry Report.

teachers, and (c) more often succeed in school than control-group children?

2. What was the relative influence of Treatment Group Membership, Entering Child Characteristics, and Home Environment Factors on child outcomes?

3. Did boys and girls in the experimental group benefit differentially from the preschool experience?

4. Did experimental-group children in different waves (replications) benefit differentially from preschool?

5. Did Entering Child Characteristics have *different* effects on outcome measures in the experimental and control groups?

6. Did Home Environment Factors have *different* effects on outcome measures in the experimental and control groups?

In addition to these basic issues, three other questions were also addressed:

7. Were test performance, teacher ratings, or School Success different for boys and girls in the total sample (controlling for group membership and wave)?

8. Did outcomes vary for children in different waves (controlling for group membership and sex)?

9. Did parents in the experimental group evidence more developmentally supportive attitudes and behaviors toward their children than parents in the control group?

The question of overall sex differences was addressed because of widespread interest in developmental differences between boys and girls; the question of wave differences was addressed because of its implications for experimental design. Long-term goals of the preschool intervention—to reduce school drop-out and delinquency and to improve adult socioeconomic status—will be evaluated in the continuing longitudinal study.

Findings for the preschool period (FEY-S2Y)

Preschool findings focus on the concurrent effects of the experimental treatment. Results obtained using conventional analysis of variance techniques are the same as those presented in the 1970 Perry Report with minor exceptions which will be noted when appropriate. The results obtained using multiple linear regression techniques are not comparable with the regression results presented in the previous report because of major differences in analytic designs. Findings presented in this section are organized around the series of research questions stated. Specific analytic designs and procedures are referenced as each question is addressed; detailed descriptions of the statistical methods applied to each question are presented in appendix B.

■ *Question 1:* **Did experimental-group children who attended preschool score higher on standardized aptitude tests than control-**

group children who did not attend preschool? (Analysis by conventional three-way analysis of variance and multiple linear regression techniques.)

Findings

Children who attended preschool scored significantly and substantially higher than control-group children on standardized aptitude tests administered in the spring of their first and second preschool years (SEY and S2Y).

Discussion

Two methods of analysis were used to address this question: conventional analysis of variance and multiple linear regression. Three-way analyses of variance (ANOVA) were performed to replicate analyses reported in the 1970 Perry Report. The ANOVA designs incorporated three factors—Treatment Group, Wave, and Sex—and their interactions. Multiple linear regression was used in order to control for both continuous and categorical independent variables in tests of the treatment main effect. The regression designs incorporated the dichotomous treatment-group variable and two sets of continuous variables: Entering Child Characteristics (FEY Binet, FEY PPVT/R, FEY ITPA/R, and FEY Leiter/R) and Home Environment Factors (Mother's Education, SES, FEY MAI/R, CHES1/R, and CHES2/R). Both methods are described in more detail in appendix B. The results obtained using each method are presented separately below.

ANOVA results.   The question was first addressed using conventional three-way analysis of variance techniques. The group main effect was tested with the effects of Sex, Wave, and all interactions of Group, Sex, and Wave statistically controlled. Although the experimental group was expected to score higher than the control group, the significance levels reported in Table 8 are for nondirectional F tests, commonly used in reporting ANOVA results.

Table 8 compares the performance of experimental and control children on all standardized aptitude tests administered during the preschool period. Of tests given at FEY, only the Binet was a true pre-measure independent of treatment, having been administered prior to project enrollment; there was no significant difference between experimental and control groups on the initial Binet.

FEY scores on the Leiter, PPVT, and ITPA were obtained up to three months after treatment had begun and must be considered dependent variables. All three variables significantly differentiated the experimental from the control group at FEY.[17] Since children in the two treatment groups seem to have been comparable prior to project enrollment (see "The sample", chapter I), these findings of differences favoring the ex-

---

[17]In the 1970 Perry Report, no significant difference appeared on the FEY ITPA total score due to slight errors in the original data file. Of the nine ITPA subtests, only the AVAS

Table 8

Comparison of Treatment-Group Means
and Results of F Tests on the Group Main Effect
for the Preschool Period

INSTRUMENT	TESTPOINTS		
	FEY	SEY	S2Y
BINET	E>C	E>C ***	E>C ***
LEITER	E>C **	E>C ***	E>C ***
PPVT	E>C **	E>C ***	E>C ***
ITPA-TOTAL	E>C *	——	E>C ***
ITPA-AVAS	E>C **	——	E>C ***

More complete results are presented in the *Statistical
Supplement*, Part A, Tables 1a-13a.

*Asterisks indicate significance level (*p<.10; **p<.05;
***p<.01). If no asterisks appear, the difference is not
significant at or beyond the .10 level.*

perimental group indicate that the preschool experience had an immediate and powerful effect on children's performance in standardized
test situations. This interpretation is supported by data obtained from
Wave 5 children[18] to whom the Binet was administered just prior to
enrollment and again three months later. Both experimental and control
children in Wave 5 had pretreatment Binet means of 75. Three months
into the program, experimental children scored significantly higher
(p<.05) than children in the control group.

The differences between experimental and control children became
even more dramatic by the end of the first preschool year and persisted
through the second. At SEY and S2Y, experimental children scored significantly higher (p<.01) than control children on all aptitude indices.
Moreover, the concurrent effects of preschool were large, in addition to
being statistically significant. Estimated percentages of variance in test
scores explained by the treatment variable ranged from 13% (PPVT) to
30% (Leiter) at SEY and from 14% (Leiter) to 33% (ITPA-AVAS) at S2Y

(Auditory Vocal Association) subtest was considered in the 1970 report. This decision was
reached on the basis of longitudinal analyses indicating that only the ITPA-AVAS consistently differentiated the experimental from the control group during both preschool and
post-treatment periods. Although the same format is followed in the body of this report,
analysis of variance results for all subtests are presented in Part A, Tables 5-13 of the
Statistical Supplement.

[18]Wave 5 children were "junior preschoolers" (three-year-olds) to Wave 4 during its final
project year. Since the experimental children in Wave 5 did not complete two years at the
Perry Preschool, they were not included in the project sample. However, their first preschool
year was comparable to that of the other waves.

(see Table 16).[19] Treatment-group means and change scores over test intervals during the preschool period are presented in Table 9. It is important to note that, assuming group differences in FEY PPVT, FEY ITPA, and FEY Leiter to be the result of several months of treatment rather than entering differences in children, control-group means at FEY are the best estimates of what experimental-group means would have looked like had all tests been administered prior to the initiation of treatment. Thus, it seems very likely that experimental-group gains on the Leiter, PPVT, and ITPA would have been substantially larger if true pre-measures had been obtained.

Regression results. The hypothesis that experimental-group children would out-perform control-group children on tests of aptitude during the preschool period was also tested using multiple linear regression techniques to predict Binet scores at SEY and S2Y from Treatment Group

Table 9

Arithmetic Means and Change Scores for Measures of Academic Potential by Treatment Group

Preschool Period

VARIABLE	GROUP	FEY	FEY-SEY CHANGE	SEY	SEY-S2Y CHANGE	S2Y	FEY-S2Y CHANGE
BINET	EXP	79.6	+15.9	95.5	−0.6	94.9	+15.3
	CON	78.5	+ 4.8	83.3	+0.2	83.5	+ 5.0
LEITER[1]	EXP	69.6	+27.4	97.0	−7.2	89.8	+20.2
	CON	59.0	+13.0	72.0	+5.9	77.9	+18.9
PPVT[1]	EXP	66.8	+ 7.7	74.5	+6.5	81.0	+14.2
	CON	62.4	+ 1.2	63.6	−0.7	62.9	+ 0.5
ITPA-TOTAL[1]	EXP	2.83	——	——	——	4.75	+ 1.92
	CON	2.62	——	——	——	3.95	+ 1.33
ITPA-AVAS[1]	EXP	2.91	——	——	——	4.42	+ 1.51
	CON	2.66	——	——	——	3.44	+ 0.78

[1]FEY Leiter, PPVT, and ITPA tests were administered up to three months after treatment had begun. See discussion of group differences in text.

Asterisks indicate significance level (*p<.10; **p<.05; ***p<.01). If no asterisks appear, the difference is not significant at or beyond the .10 level.

[19]The magnitude of experimental effects was estimated in the following manner (Blalock, 1960, p. 267):

$$E^2 = \frac{\text{between groups sum of squares}}{\text{total sum of squares}}$$

Although E^2 slightly overestimates the proportion of variance in the criterion explained by the experimental treatment, more precise estimates did not seem warranted for two reasons. First, our interest was in whether observed effects were "large" or "small", not "larger" or "smaller" than in some other experiment. Second, it is computationally difficult, if not impossible (Vaughan and Corballis, 1969), to obtain unbiased estimates, particularly in factorial designs with unequal cell sizes. Estimates obtained in this manner for the Binet (23% at SEY and 20% at S2Y) are very similar to estimates derived from regression analyses presented in Table 10.

Membership, covarying on Entering Child Characteristics and Home Environment Factors. Directional F tests were computed.

Treatment Group Membership (EXP/CON) accounted for a significant (p<.01) amount of variance in SEY and S2Y Binet scores with the experimental group scoring higher than the control group. The magnitude of the group main effect, over and above Entering Child Characteristics and Home Environment Factors, was large, explaining 24% of the variance in SEY Binet and 22% in S2Y Binet (Table 10).

■ *Question 2:* **What was the relative influence of Treatment Group Membership, Entering Child Characteristics, and Home Environment Factors on Binet performance? (Analysis by multiple linear regression; each main effect was tested over and above the other two.)**

Findings

Treatment Group Membership was by far the most powerful predictor of children's scores on Binet tests administered at SEY and S2Y.

Discussion

The relative importance of Group, Entering Child Characteristics, and Home Environment Factors in predicting preschool-period Binet performance was examined. Of the three predictor variable sets in the regression design, Treatment Group Membership was by far the most powerful predictor of Binet scores during the preschool period, explaining 24% of the variance in SEY Binet and 22% of the variance in S2Y Binet (Table 10). These effects are of the same order of magnitude as those obtained in the conventional (Group x Sex x Wave) analysis of variance design. Entering Child Characteristics (the joint effect of FEY Binet, FEY Leiter/R, FEY ITPA/R, and FEY PPVT/R) were the next most important predictors, accounting for 13% of the variance (p<.01) in both SEY and S2Y Binet scores. Home Environment Factors (the joint effect of Mother's Education, SES, CHES1/R, CHES2/R, and MAI/R) were substantially less important, explaining 6% (p<.05) of the variance in SEY Binet scores and 5% (N.S.) in S2Y Binet scores. About 13% of the variance in SEY Binet scores and 3% in S2Y Binet scores explained by the joint effect of all the predictor variables (Full Model for Main Effects, Table B-2, appendix B) could not be uniquely attributed to any of the three sets of predictor variables.

■ *Question 3:* **Did boys and girls in the experimental group benefit differentially from the experimental treatment? (Analysis by conventional analysis of variance; the Group x Sex interaction was tested with the main effects of Group, Sex, and Wave and Group x Wave, Sex x Wave, and Group x Sex x Wave interactions statistically controlled.)**

Table 10

Main Effects of Treatment Group Membership, Entering Child Characteristics, and Home Environment Factors upon Criterion Measures Obtained during the Preschool Period.

		PREDICTORS			
CRITERION MEASURES	Proportion of Variance in Criterion Measures Explained by Full Regression Model R^2_f	Treatment Group[1]		Child Characteristics[2]	Environmental Factors[2]
		Magnitude of Effect Over and Above Other Predictors R^2_f-$R^2_{r(a)}$	Magnitude of Effects Direction of Difference E/C	Magnitude of Effect Over and Above Other Predictors R^2_f-$R^2_{r(b)}$	Magnitude of Effect Over and Above Other Predictors R^2_f-$R^2_{r(c)}$
SEY BINET (N=98)	.56	.24***	E > C	.13***	.06**
S2Y BINET (N=77)	.43	.22***	E > C	.13***	.05

[1]A directional F test was used to determine the statistical significance of the group effect.

[2]Nondirectional F tests were used to determine the statistical significance of the effects of child characteristics and environmental factors.

Asterisks indicate significance level (*p<.10; **6<.05; ***p<.01). If no asterisks appear, the difference is not significant at or beyond the .10 level.

Findings

No evidence was found that boys and girls in the experimental group benefited differentially from the preschool experience.

Discussion

In analysis of 31 dependent measures[20], the only significant Group x Sex interaction was found on one of the ITPA subtests not considered in the body of this report. Nondirectional F tests were computed. Cell means and F ratios for Group x Sex interactions are presented in the *Statistical Supplement*, Part A, Tables 1b through 13b (Binet, Leiter, PPVT, and ITPA) and Tables 27b through 29b (MAI and CHES).

■ *Question 4:* **Did experimental-group children in different waves (replication samples) benefit differentially from preschool? (Analysis by conventional analysis of variance; the Group x Wave interaction was tested with the main effects of Group, Sex, and Wave and Group x Sex, Sex x Wave, and Group x Sex x Wave interactions statistically controlled.)**

Findings

There was no indication of consistent differences among experimental-group children belonging to different waves, suggesting that the evolu-

---

[20]Dependent measures analyzed: FEY PPVT, FEY Leiter, FEY ITPA (10 scales); SEY Binet, SEY PPVT, SEY Leiter, SEY MAI; S2Y Binet, S2Y PPVT, S2Y Leiter, S2Y ITPA (10 scales); CHES1, CHES2.

tion of the preschool program from year to year had no systematic effect on child outcomes.

Discussion[21]

In analyses of 31 dependent measures, only five significant Group x Wave interactions were found: three on ITPA subtests not dealt with in this (or the previous) report; one in Leiter scores at SEY; and one in CHES-Factor 1 scores. Nondirectional F tests were computed. Visual inspection of Group x Wave cell means did not reveal a consistent pattern of effects across instruments or data collection points (cf., *Statistical Supplement*, Part A, Tables 1b-13b and 27b-29b).

- *Question 5:* **Did children's entering levels of academic aptitude (Entering Child Characteristics) have different effects on Binet performance *within* the experimental and control groups? (Analysis by multiple linear regression; the interaction of Group with Entering Child Characteristics was tested over and above the effects of Group, Entering Child Characteristics, Home Environment Factors, and the interaction of Group with Home Environment Factors.)**

Findings

Entering Child Characteristics had the same effects on SEY and S2Y Binet performance within both groups.

Discussion

The interaction between Group and Entering Child Characteristics did not reach significance for either SEY or S2Y Binet predictions, indicating that the effects of Entering Child Characteristics were the same for both treatment groups (Table 11). Nondirectional F tests were computed.

- *Question 6:* **Did Home Environment Factors have different effects on Binet performance *within* the experimental and control groups? (Analysis by multiple linear regression; the interaction of Group with Home Environment Factors was tested over and above the effects of Group, Home Environment Factors, Entering Child Characteristics, and the interaction of Entering Child Characteristics with Group.)**

---

[21]Group x Wave interactions were not considered in the 1970 Perry Report since Wave had been included in the analysis of variance design solely as a blocking factor to increase the precision of tests of the Group and Sex main effects and their interaction.

Table 11

Effects of Interactions of Treatment Group Membership with Entering Child Characteristics and Home Environment Factors upon Criterion Measures Obtained during the Preschool Period

CRITERION MEASURES	Proportion of Variance in Criterion Measures Explained by Full Regression Model R^2_f	Group x Child Characteristics		Group x Environmental Factors	
		Magnitude of Effect Over and Above the Group x Environmental Factors Interaction $R^2_f - R^2_{r(d)}$	Relative Magnitude of Effects Across Groups[1] E/C	Magnitude of Effect Over and Above the Group x Child Characteristics Interaction $R^2_f - R^2_{r(e)}$	Relative Magnitude of Effects Across Groups[1] E/C
SEY BINET (N=98)	.61	.04	——	.01	——
S2Y BINET (N=77)	.47	.03	——	.03	——

[1]The relative magnitude of effects across groups is reported only when interactions reach significance at the .10 level or better. A nondirectional F test was used to determine the statistical significance of the Group x Entering Child Characteristics interaction; a directional F test, to determine the significance of the Group x Home Environment Factors interaction (see text).

Asterisks indicate significance level (*p<.10; **p<.05; ***p<.01). If no asterisks appear, the difference is not significant at or beyond the .10 level.

Findings

Home Environment Factors had the same effects on SEY and S2Y Binet performance within both treatment groups.

Discussion

Home Environment Factors might influence children's Binet performance more in the control than in the experimental group. Thus, directional F tests were computed.

The Group x Home Environment Factors interaction did not reach statistical significance (Table 11), indicating that Home Environment Factors had the same effects on SEY and S2Y Binet in both treatment groups.

- ■ *Question 7:* **In the total sample, were outcomes different for boys and girls? (Analysis by conventional analysis of variance; the Sex main effect was tested with the effects of Group, Wave, and all interactions of Group, Sex, and Wave statistically controlled.)**

Findings

Although boys tended to score higher than girls on standardized aptitude tests at SEY and S2Y, on the whole these differences were neither large nor statistically significant.

Discussion

Sex-of-child was included in the analysis of variance design because of its demonstrated correlation with many behavioral measures. Although Sex was originally considered a blocking factor in the analysis of variance, questions of sex-related differences in standardized test performance are of sufficiently wide interest to warrant brief mention here.

Only one significant difference ($p < .10$ in a nondirectional F test) between boys and girls emerged: boys scored significantly higher than girls on the SEY Leiter (Table 12). When all ITPA subtests were analyzed

Table 12

*Comparison of Sex Means
and the Results of F Tests on the Sex Main Effects
for the Preschool Period*

INSTRUMENT	TESTPOINTS		
	FEY	SEY	S2Y
BINET	B<G	B<G	B>G
LEITER	B<G	B>G*	B>G
PPVT	B<G	B>G	B>G
ITPA-TOTAL	B>G	——	B>G
ITPA-AVAS	B=G	——	B>G

More complete results are presented in the *Statistical Supplement*, Part A, Tables 1a-13a.

Asterisks indicate significance level (*p<.10; **p<.05; ***p<.01). If no asterisks appear, the difference is not significant at or beyond the .10 level.

for this report, one additional difference ($p < .05$) was found, boys scoring higher than girls (see the *Statistical Supplement*, Part A, Table 6a). Although boys clearly tend to score higher than girls after FEY, the near absence of statistically significant findings casts some doubt on the replicability of this pattern. Moreover, sex-of-child was not a very effective blocking factor since it did little to reduce error term variance in the analyses of variance of preschool-period data.

- *Question 8:* **In the total sample, did outcomes vary by waves (replication samples)? (Analysis by conventional analysis of variance; the total sample Wave effects were tested with the effects of Group, Sex, and all interactions of Group, Sex, and Wave statistically controlled.)**

Findings

Although the overall pattern of differences among waves was not consistent, Wave 4 children tended to perform at substantially higher levels than other children on all standardized measures of aptitude at SEY and S2Y.

Discussion

Wave main effects are examined both to explore the problem of sampling error in small-scale experimental replications and to evaluate the effectiveness of Wave as a "blocking factor" in the analysis of variance design. Even though great care was taken to achieve homogeneity among waves, significant Wave main effects appeared fairly consistently for all dependent measures of aptitude during the preschool period (*Statistical Supplement*, Tables 1a-13a). Although the pattern of differences was not consistent overall, Wave 4 children tended to perform at substantially higher levels than other children on all measures at all testpoints after FEY. Granted the finding of total sample Wave differences has no intrinsic interest, it clearly illustrates the difficulty of drawing comparable small samples from the same population even over short periods of time. These findings indicate that wave-of-child was an effective blocking factor by virtue of its large, independent, albeit largely unsystematic, contribution to variance in the criterion measures.

Another issue should be addressed at this juncture. It was suspected that CHES scores might have been systematically affected by wave-of-child since children in different waves were of different ages when their mothers were interviewed. Revisions in the instrument, however, seem to have eliminated this problem. No significant Wave main effects appeared for either CHES factor.

> ■ *Question 9:* **Did parents in the experimental group evidence more developmentally supportive childrearing attitudes and behaviors than parents in the control group? (Analysis by conventional analysis of variance; the Group main effect was tested with the effects of Sex and Wave and all interactions of Group, Sex, and Wave statistically controlled.)**

Findings

Although there was some suggestion that maternal childrearing *attitudes* may have been affected by the home-teaching component of the experimental treatment, no evidence of differences was found in childrearing *behaviors* reported by parents.

Discussion

Although MAI (FEY and SEY) and CHES variables were not analyzed as dependent measures in the 1970 Perry Report, they were incorporated as independent variables in regression analyses predicting child outcomes. Since neither the MAI (FEY) nor the CHES were true pre-measures and since they might reasonably have been affected by the experimental treatment (parent program), brief consideration of both instruments as parent-outcome measures seems warranted. The hypothesis of differences in parental childrearing behaviors was tested.

A marginally significant ($p < .10$) difference in MAI scores favoring experimental-group mothers appeared at FEY (Table 13a). This difference had increased slightly by SEY. Although it seems likely that the higher (more "middle class") scores of experimental-group mothers were the result of treatment rather than pre-existing differences between groups, the magnitude of any treatment effect was small, accounting for less than 3% of the variance in FEY MAI scores and less than 6% at SEY. If it is assumed that FEY differences were *not* due to treatment and MAI scores at SEY are adjusted by covarying on scores at FEY, differences between mothers in the two groups disappear (Table 13b). CHES scores on Factor 1 (Home as Learning Environment) and Factor 2 (Parent as Teacher) were not significantly different for the two treatment groups (Table 14). In short, although the experimental treatment may have had some effect on the childrearing attitudes which mothers claimed to embrace, it had no apparent effect on the actual childrearing behaviors (whether direct interaction or environmental manipulation) reported by parents on the CHES.

Findings for the post-treatment period (SKG-S4G)

Post-treatment findings focus on the longitudinal effects of the experimental treatment. This report substantially extends the longitudinal study, analyzing data obtained on all children through fourth grade, whereas data analysis in the 1970 Perry Report was restricted to Waves 0-3 at SKG, Waves 0-2 at S1G, Waves 0 and 1 at S2G, and Wave 0 alone at S3G. Given differences in the samples for which data were analyzed after S2Y and modifications in the regression design for this report, no systematic comparison of current findings with those presented in the previous report will be attempted. The presentation of findings is organized around the same research questions as were addressed in the previous section. (Questions 8 and 9 are not addressed in this section. Question 8 was covered in the analysis of preschool-period data in the preceding section. No data pertaining to question 9 were collected during the post-treatment period through fourth grade).

■ *Question 1a:* **Did experimental-group children who attended preschool score higher than control-group children on aptitude and achievement measures and teachers' ratings of academic potential administered after treatment had terminated? (Analysis by conventional analysis of variance and multiple linear regression techniques.)**

Table 14

Summary of Cognitive Home Environment Scale Analysis of Variance Results

A. CHES—Factor 1: Home As Learning Environment

ANOVA FACTOR (N=112)	F Ratio	Sig. Level
Treatment Group	<1	N.S.
Sex	<1	N.S.
Wave	<1	N.S.
Group x Sex	<1	N.S.
Group x Wave	1.91	N.S.
Sex x Wave	<1	N.S.
Group x Sex x Wave	<1	N.S.

B. CHES—Factor 2: Parent as Teacher

ANOVA FACTOR (N=112)	F Ratio	Sig. Level
Treatment Group	<1	N.S.
Sex	<1	N.S.
Wave	<1	N.S.
Group x Sex	<1	N.S.
Group x Wave	2.11	$p<.10$
Sex x Wave	<1	N.S.
Group x Sex x Wave	1.06	N.S.

More detailed results are presented in the *Statistical Supplement*, Part A, Tables 28a-c and 29a-c.

Table 13

Maternal Attitude Inventory Analysis of Variance and Analysis of Covariance Results

A. MAI Three-Way Analysis of Variance Results[1] at FEY and SEY

ANOVA FACTOR	FEY (N=115) F Ratio	FEY (N=115) Sig. Level	SEY (N=91) F Ratio	SEY (N=91) Sig. Level
Treatment Group	2.77	$p<.10$	5.34	$p<.05$
Sex	<1	N.S.	<1	N.S.
Wave	1.56	N.S.	3.02	$p<.05$
Group x Sex	1.96	N.S.	2.39	N.S.
Group x Wave	<1	N.S.	<1	N.S.
Sex x Wave	<1	N.S.	<1	N.S.
Group x Sex x Wave	<1	N.S.	1.22	N.S.

B. MAI Three-Way Analysis of Covariance[2] at SEY Covarying on FEY Scores

ANCOVA FACTOR	F Ratio	Sig. Level
Treatment Group	<1	N.S.
Sex	1.88	N.S.
Wave	1.13	N.S.
Group x Sex	1.68	N.S.
Group x Wave	2.01	N.S.
Sex x Wave	<1	N.S.

[1] More detailed results are presented in the *Statistical Supplement*, Part A, Tables 27a-27c.

[2] The analysis of covariance was performed using Overall and Spiegel's (1969) least squares regression method #2 and incorporating the covariate (MAI at FEY) in the regression model as suggested by Cohen (1968). The Group x Sex x Wave interaction was collapsed into the error term.

Findings

Children from the experimental group consistently evidenced somewhat higher scores than children in the control group on aptitude and achievement measures and teacher ratings of academic potential obtained at SKG through S4G.

1. On *aptitude* measures the magnitude of differences tended to decrease once treatment terminated and all children entered elementary school. In spite of this overall trend, however, statistically significant differences favoring the experimental group did persist through third grade on certain measures.

2. On *achievement* measures the magnitude of differences tended to increase as the children experienced elementary education.

3. On *teacher ratings of academic potential* the experimental children were consistently but not significantly rated higher.

Discussion

Two methods of analysis were used to address this question: conventional analysis of variance (ANOVA) and multiple linear regression. Specific analytic designs are described fully in appendix B. The results obtained using each method are presented separately below.

ANOVA results.   Question 1a was first addressed using conventional three-way analysis of variance techniques. The Group main effect was tested with the effects of Sex, Wave, and all interactions of Group, Sex, and Wave statistically controlled. Although the experimental group was expected to score higher than the control group, the significance levels reported in Table 15 are from nondirectional F tests, most commonly used in reporting ANOVA results.

The pattern of differences in mean scores in measures of aptitude and achievement is strikingly consistent from SKG through S4G, favoring the experimental group in every instance (Table 15). It is highly unlikely $(p<.0000001)$ that this pattern occurred by chance.[22] However, the magnitude of the treatment effect diminished substantially after the experimental treatment terminated (Table 16). Figures 1 through 5 clearly illustrate the contrast between the preschool and post-treatment (elementary school) periods.

In the spring of their second preschool year (S2Y), the average Binet score of experimental-group children reflected a gain of 15.3 points from FEY, or 10.3 points more than control-group children (Figure 1). One year later, in the spring of their kindergarten year, experimental-group children reflected a gain of 11.7 points from FEY, only 4 points more than

---

[22]A sign test was used to test the pattern of differences (Hays, 1963; p. 625).

Table 15

Comparison of Treatment Group Means for the Post-Treatment Period Indicating Results of F Tests from Analyses of Variance

Measures of Aptitude and Achievement

ELEMENTARY SCHOOL MEASURES	CURRENT FINDINGS				
	SKG	S1G	S2G	S3G	S4G
BINET	E>C **	E>C **	E>C	E>C	E>C
LEITER	E>C	E>C	E>C	E>C **	——
PPVT	E>C **	E>C	E>C	E>C	——
ITPA-TOTAL	E>C	E>C	E>C	E>C *	——
ITPA-AVAS	E>C **	E>C ***	E>C	E>C **	——
CAT-TOTAL	——	E>C *	E>C	E>C **	E>C **
CAT-Reading	——	E>C	E>C	E>C **	E>C **
CAT-Arithmetic	——	E>C **	E>C *	E>C *	E>C
CAT-Language	——	E>C	E>C	E>C **	E>C ***
PBI-Academic Motivation	E>C	E>C	E>C	E>C	——
YRS-Academic Potential	E>C	E>C	E>C	E>C	——
YRS-Verbal Skill	E>C	E>C	E>C ***	E>C	——

More complete results are presented in the *Statistical Supplement*, Part A, Tables 1a-4a, 8a, and 14a-17a.

Asterisks indicate significance level (*p<.10; **p<.05; ***p<.01). If no asterisks appear, the difference is not significant at or beyond the .10 level.

Table 16

Maximum Percentages of Variance in Criterion Measures Explained by the Treatment Variable

INSTRUMENT	TESTPOINTS						
	SEY (%)	S2Y (%)	SKG (%)	S1G (%)	S2G (%)	S3G (%)	S4G (%)
BINET	23	20	4	4	1	1	1
LEITER	30	14	1	1	1	4	——
PPVT	13	22	4	2	1	1	——
ITPA-TOTAL	——	27	1	2	2	3	——
ITPA-AVAS	——	33	4	9	1	4	——
CAT-TOTAL	——	——	——	3	2	4	4
PBI-AM	——	——	1	1	1	1	——
YRS-AP	——	——	1	0	1	1	——
YRS-VS	——	——	0	0	9	0	——

The magnitude of experimental effects was estimated in the following manner (Blalock, 1960; p. 264):

$$E^2 = \frac{\text{between groups sum of squares}}{\text{total sum of squares}}$$

Although E^2 slightly overestimates the proportion of variance in the criterion explained by the experimental treatment, more precise estimations did not seem warranted for two reasons. First, our interest was in whether observed effects were "large" or "small", not "larger" or "smaller" than in some other experiment. Second, it is computationally difficult, if not impossible (cf., Vaughan and Corballis, 1969), to obtain unbiased estimates, particularly in factorial designs with unequal cell sizes.

Figure 1

Average Stanford-Binet Intelligence Scale Scores
for Experimental and Control Groups

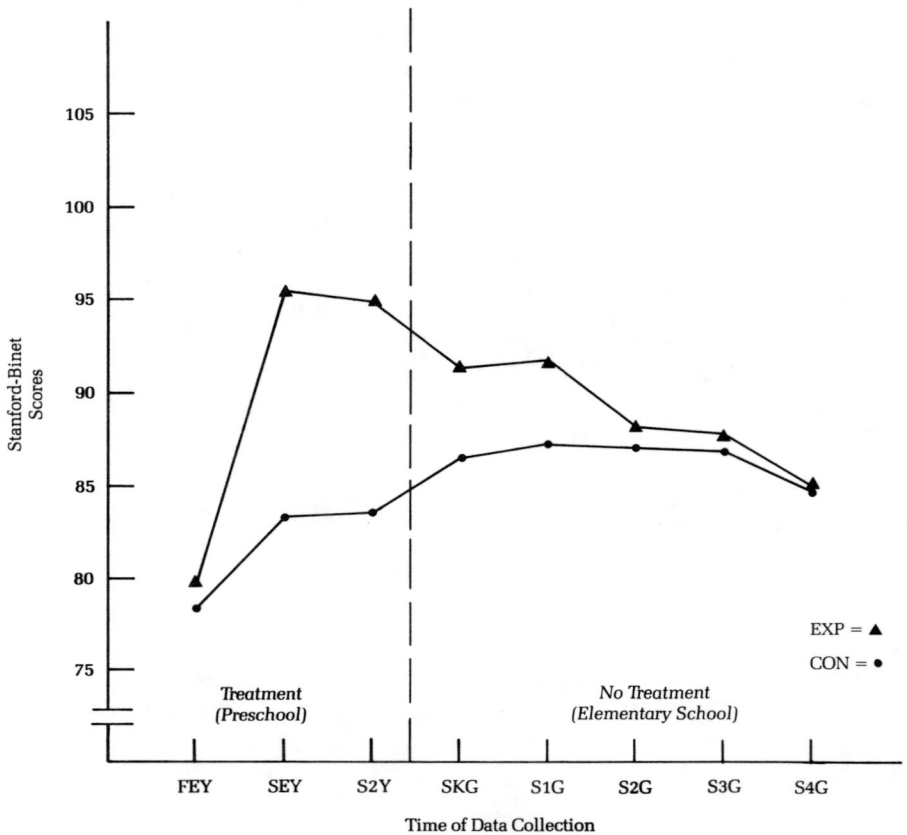

Arithmetic Means, Standard Deviations,
Number of Subjects, and Significance Levels of F Tests
on Group Comparisons at Each Testpoint

		Time of Data Collection							
		FEY	SEY	S2Y	SKG	S1G	S2G	S3G	S4G
EXP	Mean	79.6	95.5	94.9	91.3	91.7	88.1	87.7	85.0
	(S.D.)	(5.9)	(11.5)	(13.0)	(12.2)	(11.7)	(13.1)	(10.9)	(11.3)
	N	58	58	44	56	58	55	56	57
CON	Mean	78.5	83.3	83.5	86.3	87.1	86.9	86.8	84.6
	(S.D.)	(6.9)	(10.0)	(10.2)	(9.9)	(10.2)	(10.7)	(12.5)	(11.2)
	N	65	65	49	64	61	62	61	57
Significance of F tests		N.S.	<.01	<.01	<.05	<.05	N.S.	N.S.	N.S.

F tests presented here were obtained in three-way analyses of variance (Group x Sex x Wave) reported in the *Statistical Supplement*, Part A, Tables 1a-1c.

Figure 2

Average Leiter International Performance Scale Scores for Experimental and Control Groups

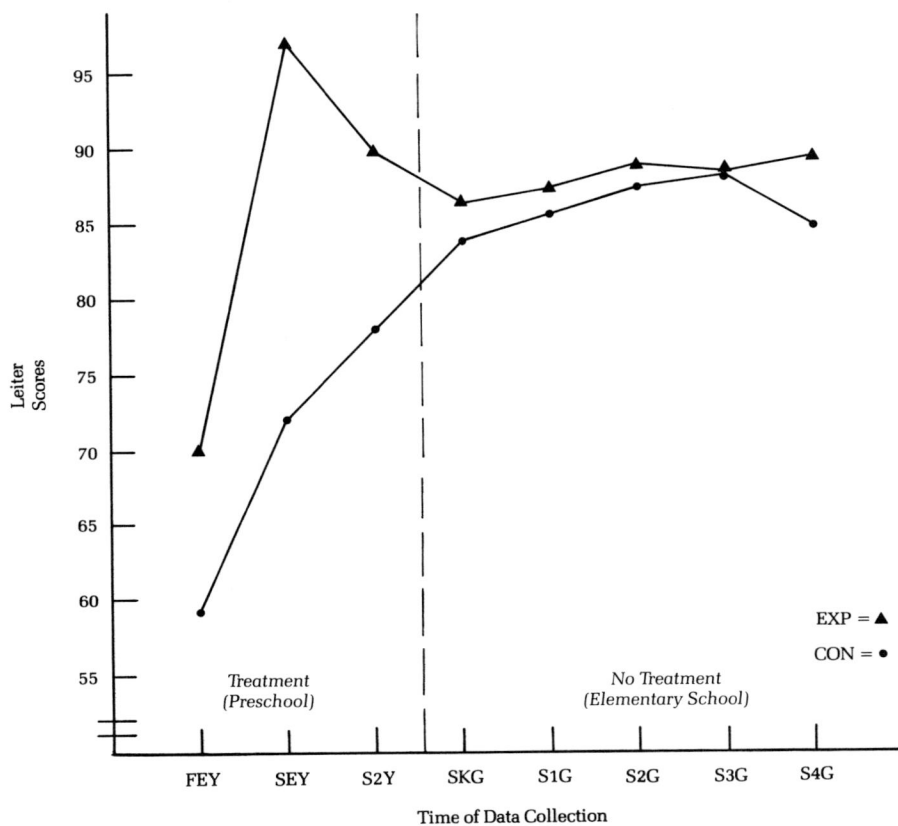

Arithmetic Means, Standard Deviations,
Number of Subjects, and Significance Levels of F Tests
on Group Comparisons at Each Testpoint

		\multicolumn{8}{c}{Time of Data Collection}							
		FEY	SEY	S2Y	SKG	S1G	S2G	S3G	S4G
EXP	Mean	69.6	97.0	89.8	86.3	88.6	88.4	89.3	——
	(S.D.)	(21.9)	(15.7)	(14.0)	(11.7)	(12.0)	(10.4)	(10.0)	——
	N	58	37	44	56	58	54	54	——
CON	Mean	59.0	72.0	77.9	83.7	87.2	88.0	84.8	——
	(S.D.)	(18.0)	(20.6)	(14.6)	(13.1)	(11.3)	(13.1)	(12.3)	——
	N	64	41	49	63	61	62	60	——
Significance of F tests		<.05	<.01	<.01	N.S.	N.S.	N.S.	<.05	——

F tests presented here were obtained in three-way analyses of variance (Group x Sex x Wave) reported in the *Statistical Supplement*, Part A, Tables 2a-2c.

52

Figure 3

Average Peabody Picture Vocabulary Test Scores for Experimental and Control Groups

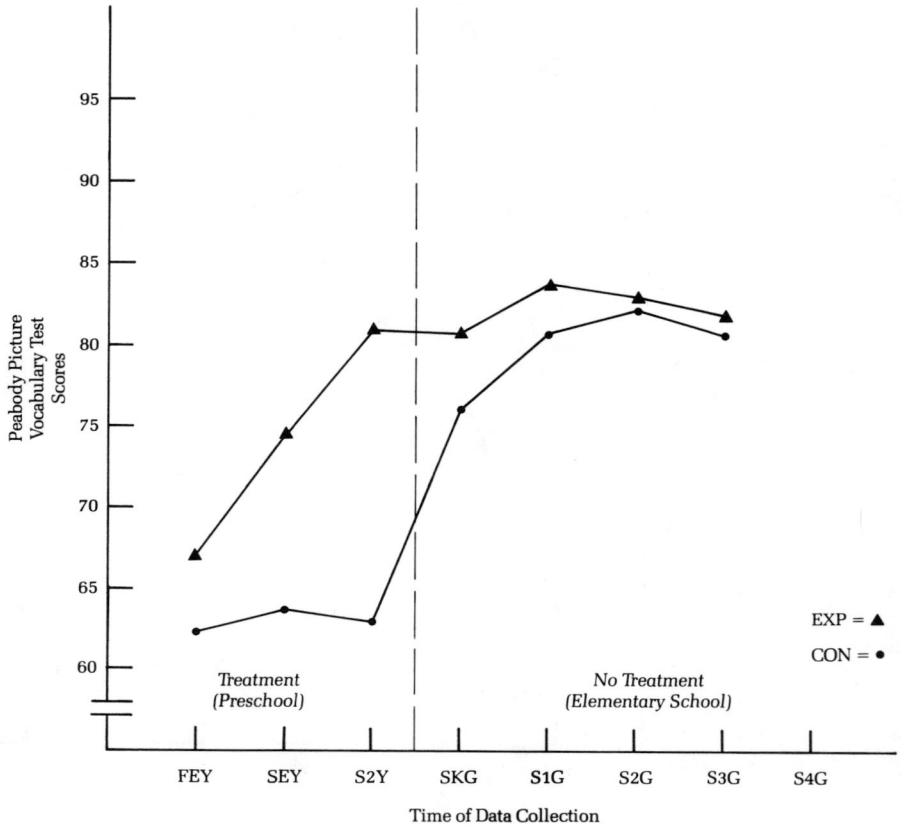

Arithmetic Means, Standard Deviations,
Number of Subjects, and Significance Levels of F Tests
on Group Comparisons at Each Testpoint

		FEY	SEY	S2Y	SKG	S1G	S2G	S3G	S4G
		\multicolumn{8}{c|}{Time of Data Collection}							
EXP	Mean	66.8	74.5	81.0	80.8	83.8	83.0	81.7	——
	(S.D.)	(12.1)	(15.6)	(20.9)	(15.7)	(12.9)	(14.7)	(13.6)	——
	N	58	37	44	56	58	55	56	——
CON	Mean	62.4	63.6	62.9	75.8	80.6	82.0	80.4	——
	(S.D.)	(8.2)	(13.1)	(15.1)	(14.2)	(12.5)	(10.3)	(14.3)	——
	N	60	41	49	64	61	61	61	——
Significance of F tests		<.05	<.01	<.01	<.05	N.S.	N.S.	N.S.	——

F tests presented here were obtained in three-way analyses of variance (Group x Sex x Wave) reported in the *Statistical Supplement*, Part A, Tables 3a-3c.

Figure 4

Average Illinois Test of Psycholinguistic Abilities
Total Scores for Experimental and Control Groups

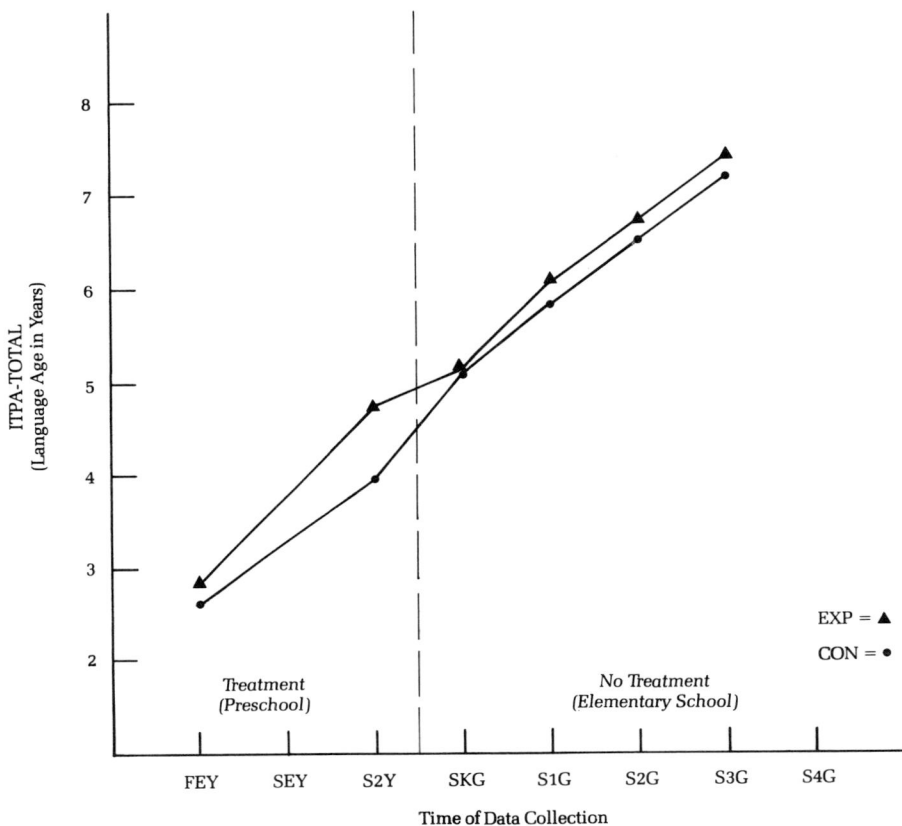

Arithmetic Means, Standard Deviations,
Number of Subjects, and Significance Levels of F Tests
on Group Comparisons at Each Testpoint

		FEY	SEY	S2Y	SKG	S1G	S2G	S3G	S4G
EXP	Mean	2.83	——	4.75	5.17	6.09	6.74	7.45	——
	(S.D.)	(0.78)	——	(0.70)	(0.69)	(0.80)	(0.94)	(1.07)	——
	N	55	——	44	55	54	48	54	——
CON	Mean	2.62	——	3.95	5.05	5.86	6.52	7.22	——
	(S.D.)	(0.72)	——	(0.56)	(0.54)	(0.60)	(0.80)	(0.92)	——
	N	65	——	47	62	54	54	56	——
Significance of F Tests		<.10	——	<.01	N.S.	N.S.	N.S.	<.10	——

F tests presented here were obtained in three-way analyses of variance (Group x Sex x Wave) reported in the *Statistical Supplement*, Part A, Tables 4a-4c.

Figure 5

*Average ITPA Auditory-Vocal Association Scores
for Experimental and Control Groups*

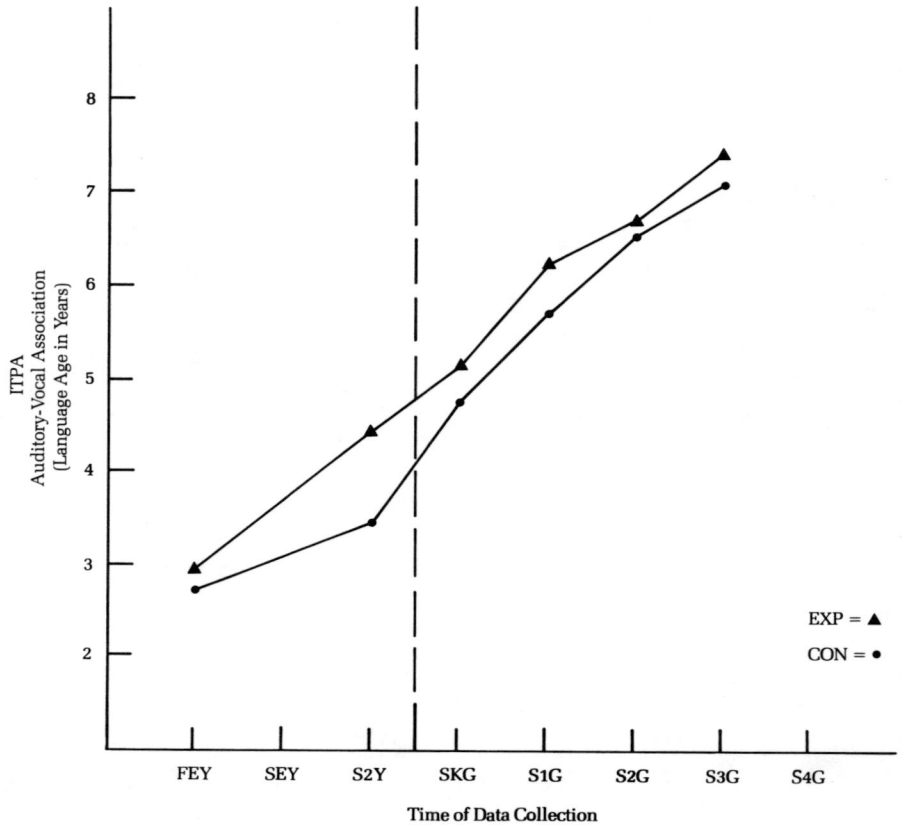

Arithmetic Means, Standard Deviations,
Number of Subjects, and Significance Levels of F Tests
on Group Comparisons at Each Testpoint

		FEY	SEY	S2Y	SKG	S1G	S2G	S3G	S4G
	Mean	2.91	——	4.42	5.14	6.23	6.70	7.42	——
EXP	(S.D.)	(0.56)	——	(0.74)	(0.90)	(0.79)	(0.79)	(0.87)	——
	N	56	——	44	55	55	50	55	——
	Mean	2.66	——	3.44	4.75	5.69	6.53	7.10	——
CON	(S.D.)	(0.54)	——	(0.62)	(0.98)	(1.08)	(0.90)	(0.77)	——
	N	65	——	47	62	56	59	56	——
Significance of F Tests		<.05	——	<.01	<.05	<.01	N.S.	<.05	——

F tests presented here were obtained in three-way analyses of variance (Group x Sex x Wave) reported in the *Statistical Supplement*, Part A, Tables 8a-8c.

control-group children who had gained additional points upon school entry. Although differences between the two groups remained significant through the first grade, the performance of experimental-group children gradually declined once they entered elementary school while children in the control group gained somewhat during kindergarten and first grade. By S4G the difference between the two groups was very small indeed. However, both control and experimental children obtained Binet test scores 6 points above FEY levels. PPVT scores evidenced a similar trend, significant differences disappearing by first grade (Figure 2). Control-group performance on the Leiter improved steadily from FEY through S2G, while experimental-group performance declined substantially from SEY through SKG (Figure 3). The only significant difference in Leiter scores obtained during the post-treatment period appeared at S4G when the experimental group evidenced a slight gain over the preceding year and the control group a somewhat larger loss. ITPA total scores (expressed in "language age") increased for children in both groups from FEY through the final administration at S3G (Figure 4). However, the rate of increase in language age of experimental-group children diminished during their kindergarten year, bringing them quite close to the performance level of children in the control group. One marginally significant difference ($p < .10$) favoring the experimental group appeared at S3G.

The Auditory-Vocal Association (verbal analogies) subscale of the ITPA and the CAT more consistently differentiated children in the two groups during the post-treatment period. Experimental-group performance on the AVAS subtest of the ITPA was significantly higher ($p < .05$ or better) than that of the control group at every testpoint except S2G (Figure 5). CAT results are particularly interesting since they suggest that differences favoring the experimental group actually *increased* during the early elementary school years (Figures 6 through 9). With the exception of the Arithmetic subtest, differences between the two groups were greater in third and fourth grades than in first and second grades. Differences in CAT total scores favoring the experimental group were marginally significant at S1G ($p < .10$), not significant at S2G, and significant at the .05 level at both S3G and S4G.

Results on the PBI-AM, YRS-AP, and YRS-VS are inconclusive (Figures 10 through 12). Although teachers rated experimental-group children consistently higher in "academic motivation", "academic potential", and "verbal skill" than children from the control group, mean ratings for the two groups were significantly different on only one of these scales at a single testpoint—Verbal Skill at S2G. The suggestion in the 1970 Perry Report that not only consistent, but reliable, differences might emerge on these scales once data were analyzed for all waves was not confirmed. Nevertheless, the consistently higher rating favoring the experimental group was maintained for the full sample.

Regression results. The hypothesis that experimental-group children would obtain higher Binet and CAT scores than children in the control group during the post-treatment period was also tested using multiple linear regression techniques. Binet scores at SKG through S4G and CAT scores at S1G through S4G were predicted by Treatment Group Membership, covarying on Entering Child Characteristics (FEY Binet, FEY

Figure 6

*Average CAT-BATTERY TOTAL Raw Scores
for Experimental and Control Groups*

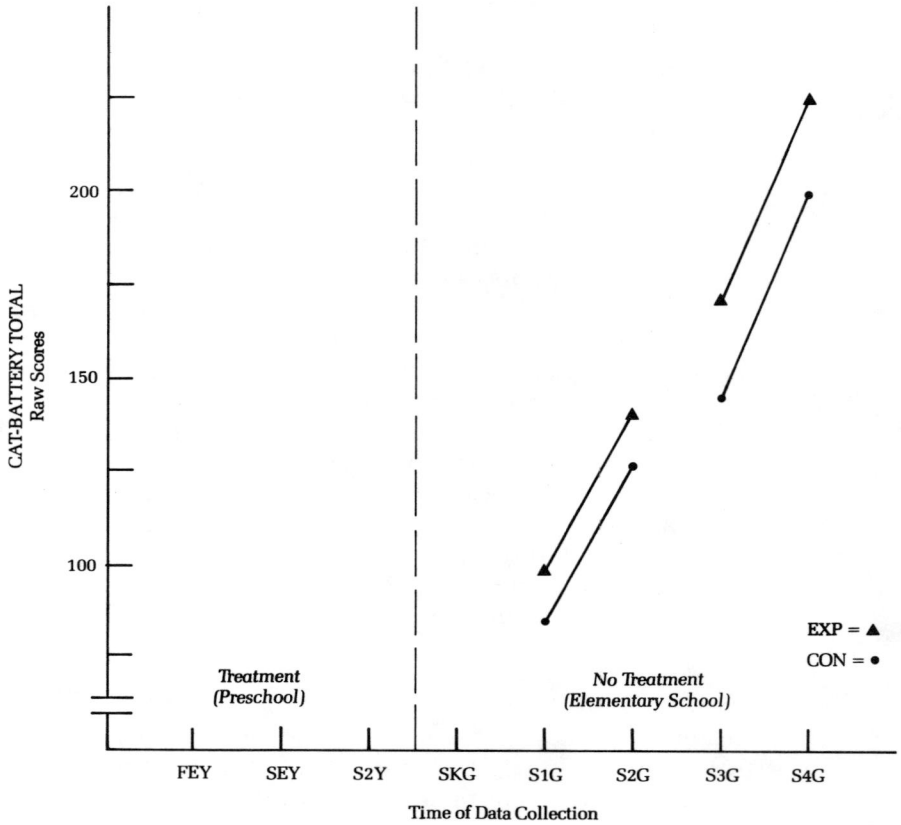

Arithmetic Means, Standard Deviations,
Number of Subjects, and Significance Levels of F Tests
on Group Comparisons at Each Testpoint

		Time of Data Collection							
		FEY	SEY	S2Y	SKG	S1G	S2G	S3G	S4G
EXP	Mean	—	—	—	—	97.1	142.6	172.8	225.5
	(S.D.)	—	—	—	—	(39.9)	(48.0)	(69.8)	(72.2)
	N	—	—	—	—	53	49	54	49
CON	Mean	—	—	—	—	84.4	126.5	145.5	199.3
	(S.D.)	—	—	—	—	(37.7)	(45.7)	(76.5)	(84.1)
	N	—	—	—	—	60	56	55	46
Significance of F Tests		—	—	—	—	$<.10$	N.S.	$<.05$	$<.05$

F tests presented here were obtained in three-way analyses of variance (Group x Sex x Wave)
reported in the *Statistical Supplement*, Part A, Tables 14a-14c.

Figure 7

*Average CAT-READING Subtest Raw Scores
for Experimental and Control Groups*

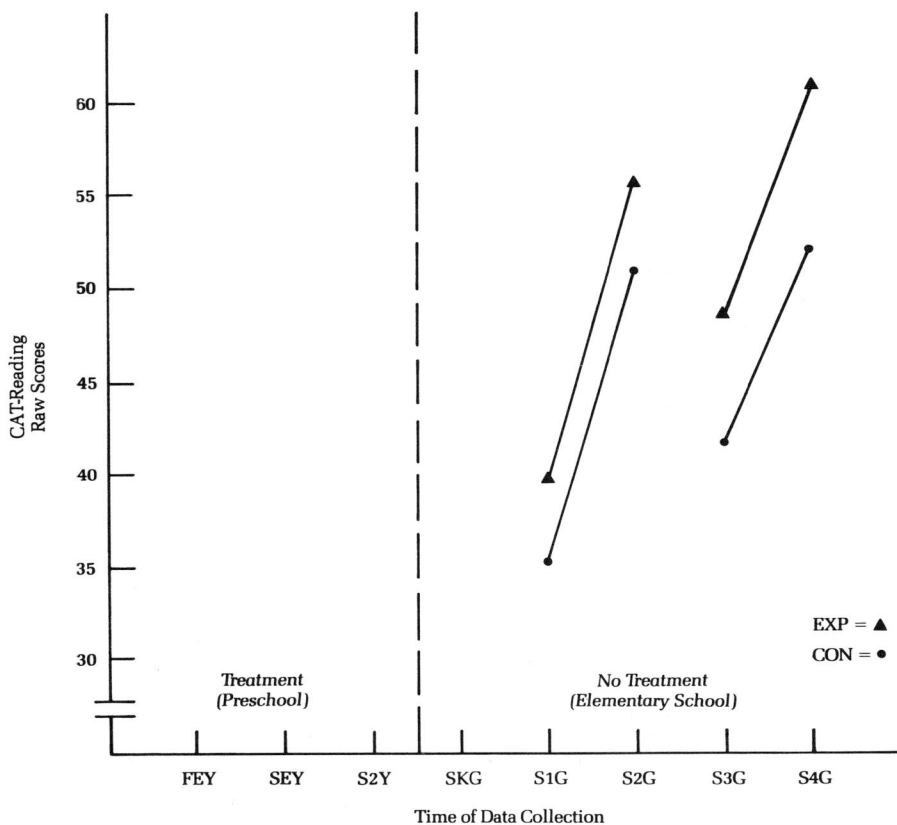

Arithmetic Means, Standard Deviations,
Number of Subjects, and Significance Levels of F Tests
on Group Comparisons at Each Testpoint

		\multicolumn{8}{c}{Time of Data Collection}							
		FEY	SEY	S2Y	SKG	S1G	S2G	S3G	S4G
EXP	Mean	——	——	——	——	39.7	56.0	48.7	60.6
	(S.D.)	——	——	——	——	(15.1)	(17.6)	(21.2)	(21.6)
	N	——	——	——	——	53	49	54	49
CON	Mean	——	——	——	——	35.3	51.2	41.9	52.3
	(S.D.)	——	——	——	——	(13.7)	(16.3)	(19.7)	(23.6)
	N	——	——	——	——	60	56	56	46
Significance of F Tests		——	——	——	——	N.S.	N.S.	<.05	<.05

F tests presented here were obtained in three-way analyses of variance (Group x Sex x Wave)
reported in the *Statistical Supplement*, Part A, Tables 15a-15c.

Figure 8

Average CAT-ARITHMETIC Subtest Raw Scores
for Experimental and Control Groups

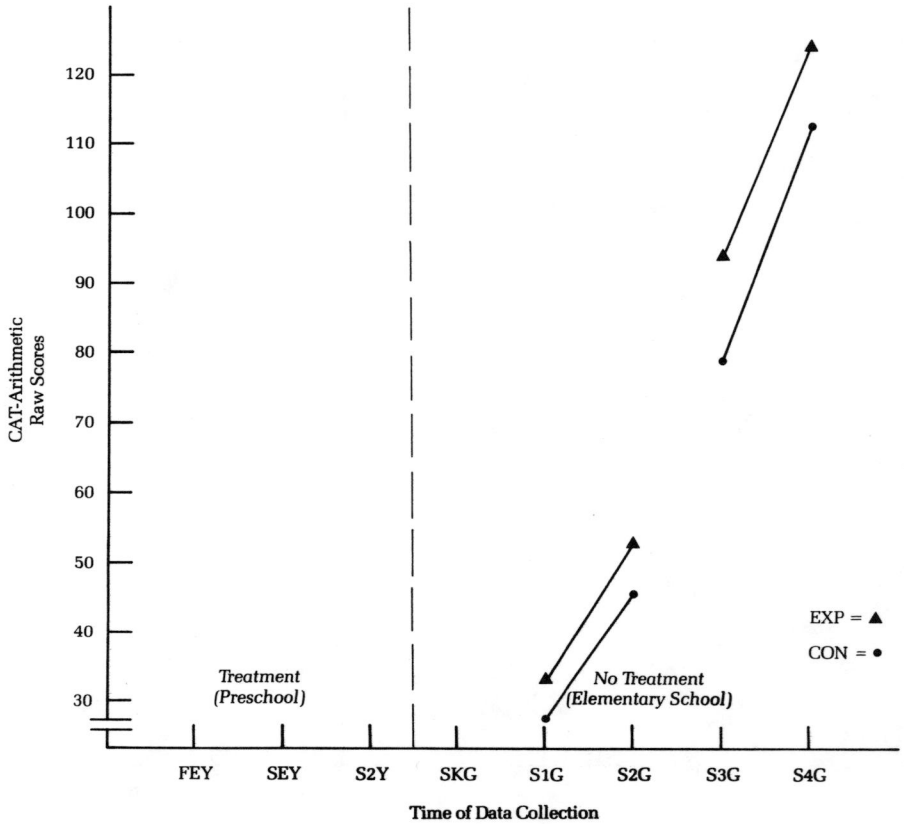

Arithmetic Means, Standard Deviations,
Number of Subjects, and Significance Levels of F Tests
on Group Comparisons at Each Testpoint

		FEY	SEY	S2Y	SKG	S1G	S2G	S3G	S4G
		\multicolumn{8}{c}{Time of Data Collection}							
EXP	Mean	—	—	—	—	32.6	53.0	93.8	124.2
	(S.D.)	—	—	—	—	(18.0)	(18.9)	(40.2)	(36.4)
	N	—	—	—	—	53	49	54	49
CON	Mean	—	—	—	—	27.0	45.3	79.0	112.4
	(S.D.)	—	—	—	—	(17.8)	(21.4)	(45.7)	(49.2)
	N	—	—	—	—	60	56	56	46
Significance of F Tests		—	—	—	—	<.05	<.10	<.10	N.S.

F tests presented here were obtained in three-way analyses of variance (Group x Sex x Wave)
reported in the *Statistical Supplement*, Part A, Tables 16a-16c.

Figure 9

*Average CAT-LANGUAGE Subtest Raw Scores
for Experimental and Control Groups*

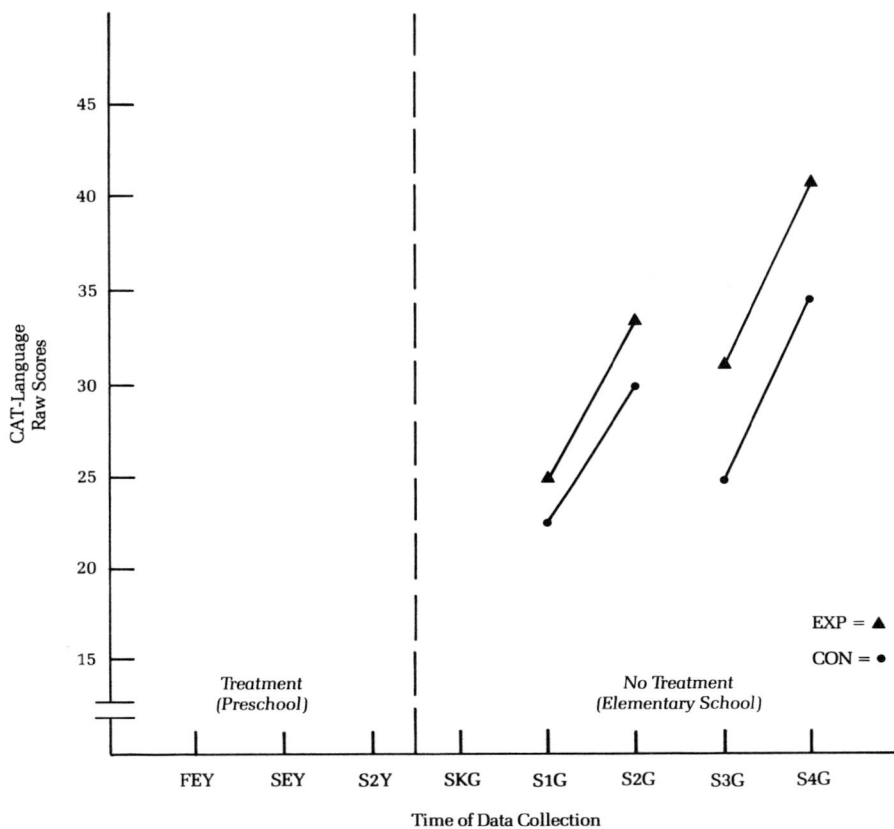

Arithmetic Means, Standard Deviations,
Number of Subjects, and Significance Levels of F Tests
on Group Comparisons at Each Testpoint

		Time of Data Collection							
		FEY	SEY	S2Y	SKG	S1G	S2G	S3G	S4G
EXP	Mean	——	——	——	——	24.9	33.5	31.0	40.9
	(S.D.)	——	——	——	——	(12.1)	(16.3)	(16.0)	(18.5)
	N	——	——	——	——	53	49	53	49
CON	Mean	——	——	——	——	22.5	30.0	24.8	34.6
	(S.D.)	——	——	——	——	(11.2)	(12.9)	(15.0)	(15.9)
	N	——	——	——	——	60	56	55	46
Significance of F Tests		——	——	——	——	N.S.	N.S.	<.05	<.01

F tests presented here were obtained in three-way analyses of variance (Group x Sex x Wave)
reported in the *Statistical Supplement*, Part A, Tables 17a-17c.

Figure 10

*Average PBI Academic Motivation Factor Scores
for Experimental and Control Groups*

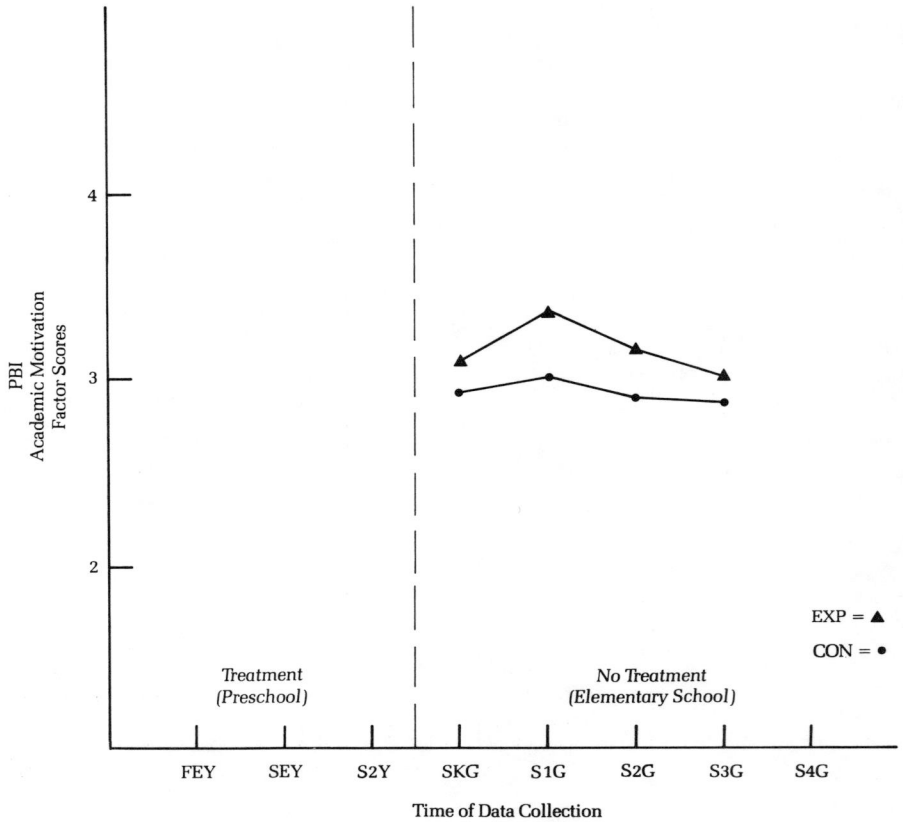

Arithmetic Means, Standard Deviations,
Number of Subjects, and Significance Levels of F Tests
on Group Comparisons at Each Testpoint

		Time of Data Collection							
		FEY	SEY	S2Y	SKG	S1G	S2G	S3G	S4G
EXP	Mean	——	——	——	3.08	3.36	3.13	3.00	——
	(S.D.)	——	——	——	(0.89)	(0.94)	(0.98)	(1.05)	——
	N	——	——	——	55	48	44	38	——
CON	Mean	——	——	——	2.91	3.00	2.89	2.87	——
	(S.D.)	——	——	——	(0.74)	(0.91)	(1.10)	(0.98)	——
	N	——	——	——	62	56	47	40	——
Significance of F Tests		——	——	——	N.S.	N.S.	N.S.	N.S.	——

F tests presented here were obtained in three-way analyses of variance (Group x Sex x Wave)
reported in the *Statistical Supplement*, Part A, Tables 18a-18c.

Figure 11

*Average YRS Academic Potential Factor Scores
for Experimental and Control Groups*

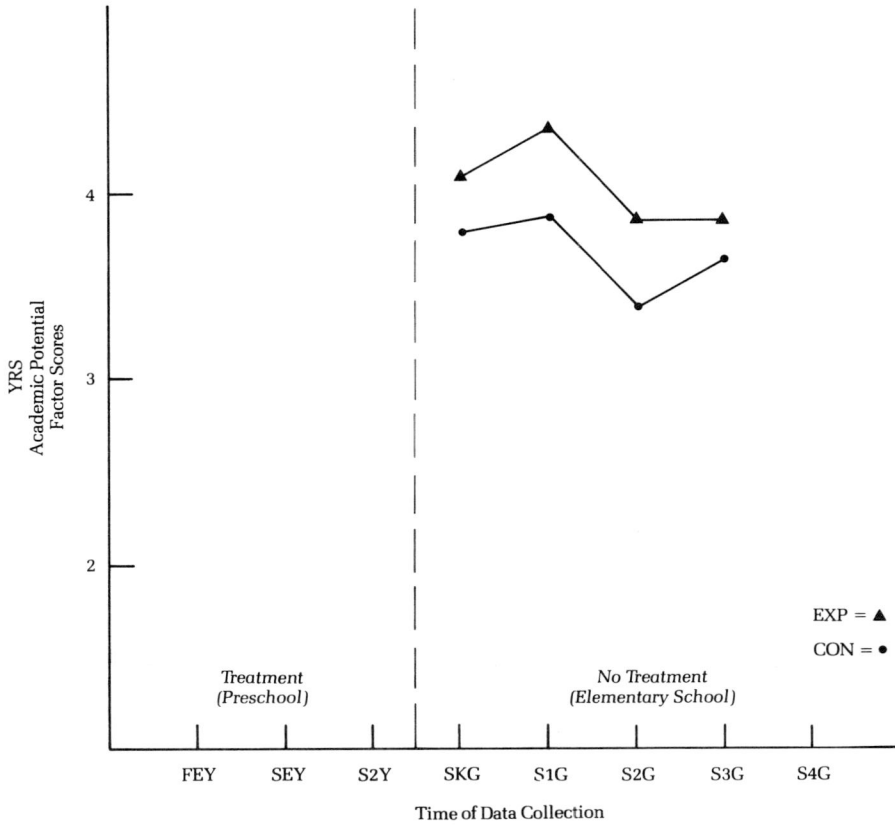

Arithmetic Means, Standard Deviations,
Number of Subjects, and Significance Levels of F Tests
on Group Comparisons at Each Testpoint

					Time of Data Collection				
		FEY	SEY	S2Y	SKG	S1G	S2G	S3G	S4G
EXP	Mean	——	——	——	4.19	4.35	3.85	3.85	——
	(S.D.)	——	——	——	(1.49)	(1.60)	(1.69)	(1.64)	——
	N	——	——	——	55	47	44	50	——
CON	Mean	——	——	——	3.80	3.86	3.38	3.64	——
	(S.D.)	——	——	——	(1.17)	(1.74)	(1.70)	(1.93)	——
	N	——	——	——	62	55	47	51	——
Significance of F Tests		——	——	——	N.S.	N.S.	N.S.	N.S.	——

F tests presented here were obtained in three-way analyses of variance (Group x Sex x Wave)
reported in the *Statistical Supplement*, Part A, Tables 19a-19c.

Figure 12

*Average YRS Verbal Skill Factor Scores
for Experimental and Control Groups*

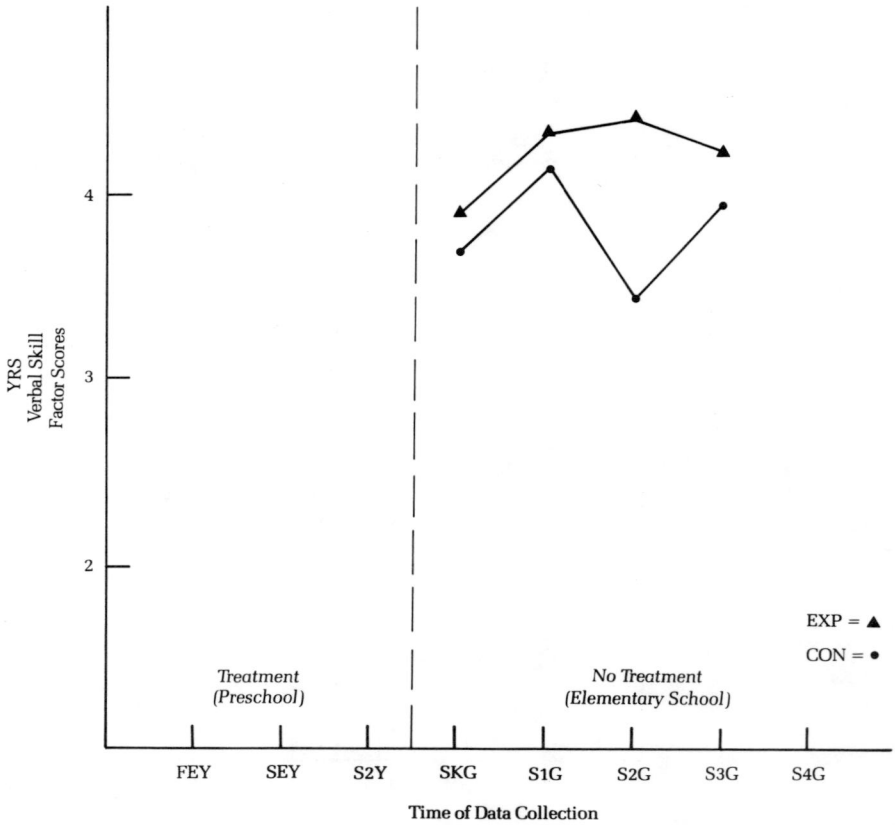

Arithmetic Means, Standard Deviations,
Number of Subjects, and Significance Levels of F Tests
on Group Comparisons at Each Testpoint

			Time of Data Collection						
		FEY	SEY	S2Y	SKG	S1G	S2G	S3G	S4G
EXP	Mean	——	——	——	3.89	4.32	4.39	4.22	——
	(S.D.)	——	——	——	(1.79)	(1.75)	(1.83)	(1.95)	——
	N	——	——	——	55	47	44	50	——
CON	Mean	——	——	——	3.68	4.23	3.43	3.94	——
	(S.D.)	——	——	——	(1.47)	(1.82)	(1.64)	(1.97)	——
	N	——	——	——	62	56	47	51	——
Significance of F Tests		——	——	——	N.S.	N.S.	<.01	N.S.	——

F tests presented here were obtained in three-way analyses of variance (Group x Sex x Wave)
reported in the *Statistical Supplement,* Part A, Tables 20a-20c.

PPVT/R, FEY ITPA/R, FEY Leiter/R) and Home Environment Factors (Mother's Education, SES, FEY MAI/R, CHES1/R, CHES2/R). Directional F tests were computed.

The findings presented in Table 17 parallel those obtained from three-way analyses of variance. Experimentals scored significantly higher than controls on the Binet at SKG and S1G. Treatment Group Membership explained 4% of the variance in SKG Binet scores and 3% at S1G. By S2G, however, no significant differences were found on the Binet, and the amount of variance in the criterion explained by Group dropped to less than 1%.

Small but persistent differences favoring the experimetal group were found in CAT-Total scores. In the standard regression design, Treatment Group Membership (over and above Entering Child Characteristics and Home Environmental Factors) accounted for marginally significant ($p < .10$) amounts of variance (1-2%) in CAT-Total scores at all testpoints.

Supplemental regression analyses, incorporating mother's employment status at FEY as an additional covariate, were also performed. At project entry, the experimental and control groups differed with respect to only one measured characteristic—proportion of working mothers: 31% of control-group mothers but only 9% of mothers in the experimental group were employed. Correlational analysis of the relationships between mother's employment status (1 = not employed; 2+ = employed) and child outcomes during the post-treatment period indicated that children of mothers who were working at FEY tended to score higher on the CAT at S2G through S4G regardless of treatment. When mother's employment status at FEY was incorporated in regression equations as a predictor of CAT-Total scores (along with Group, Entering Child Characteristics, and Home Environment Factors), the significance of experimental > control differences and the magnitude of the Group effect increased at S2G, S3G, and S4G (Table 17, bracketed proportions) to levels obtained in conventional analyses of variance (see Table 11). Indeed, these findings strongly suggest that the impact of the experimental treatment grew stronger over time, accounting for only 1% of the variance in CAT-Total scores at S1G but for 5% by S4G.[23]

- *Question 1b*: **Did elementary-school teachers consider children who had attended preschool more socially and emotionally mature than children in the control group? (Analysis by conventional analysis of variance; the Group main effect was tested with the effects of Sex, Wave, and all interactions of Group, Sex, and Wave statistically controlled.)**

Findings

Although the overall pattern of differences in average teacher ratings clearly (and significantly) favored the experimental group after kindergar-

---

[23]Preliminary analyses of achievement test data through eighth grade (S8G) indicate that the Group effect has continued to increase in magnitude.

Table 17

Main Effects of Treatment Group Membership, Entering Child Characteristics, and Home Environment Factors Obtained during the Post-Treatment Period

CRITERION MEASURES	SAMPLE SIZE N	Proportion of Variance in Criterion Measures Explained by Full Regression Model R^2_f	PREDICTORS			
			Treatment Group[1]		Child Characteristics[2]	Environmental Factors[2]
			Magnitude of Effect Over and Above Other Predictors $R^2_f - R^2_{T(a)}$	Direction of Difference E/C	Magnitude of Effect Over and Above Other Predictors $R^2_f - R^2_{T(b)}$	Magnitude of Effect Over and Above Other Predictors $R^2_f - R^2_{T(c)}$
SKG BINET	98	.42	.04***	E > C	.22***	.06
S1G BINET	95	.38	.03**	E > C	.15***	.08*
S2G BINET	93	.32	.00	—	.14***	.08
S3G BINET	92	.43	.00	—	.23***	.07*
S4G BINET	92	.31	.00	—	.12**	.09*
S1G CAT-TOTAL	90	.45	.01* [.01*][3]	E > C	.15***	.15***
S2G CAT-TOTAL	85	.36	.02* [.03**]	E > C	.05	.19***
S3G CAT-TOTAL	86	.35	.02* [.03**]	E > C	.06	.16***
S4G CAT-TOTAL	76	.36	.02* [.05**]	E > C	.04	.19***

[1]Directional F tests were used to determine the statistical significance of the Group effect.

[2]Nondirectional F tests were used to determine the statistical significance of the effects of Child Characteristics and Home Environment Factors.

[3]The proportions reported in brackets represent the magnitude of the Group main effect when one additional covariate—mother's employment status—was incorporated in the regression design. See text for discussion.

Asterisks indicate significance level (*p <.10; **p <.05; ***p <.01). If no asterisks appear, the difference is not significant at or beyond the .10 level.

ten, specific comparisons between groups were not consistently significant.

Discussion

After kindergarten, teachers tended to rate experimental-group children higher than control-group children on scales of social-emotional development from the PBI and YRS (Table 18 and Figures 13 through 18). The probability that the pattern of differences in mean ratings obtained for the entire post-treatment period could have occurred by chance was less than .01.[24] Although the direction of differences on these scales was fairly consistent, specific comparisons between the two groups reached significance only about a third of the time from SKG through S4G and 50% of the time from S1G through S4G. The suggestion in the previous report that consistently *significant* differences on these scales might be found when complete data were analyzed was not confirmed. On the other hand, it is interesting to note that differences favoring the experimental group tended to become somewhat stronger over time, contradicting the trend observed for measures of aptitude but paralleling the trend for measures of achievement.

- *Question 1c:* **Did experimental-group children achieve greater school success in the elementary grades than children in the control group? (Analysis by conventional analysis of variance and multiple linear regression techniques.)**

Table 18

Comparison of Treatment Group Means for the Post-Treatment Period Indicating Results of F Tests from Analyses of Variance[1]

Measures of Socio-Emotional Development

ELEMENTARY SCHOOL MEASURES	CURRENT FINDINGS				
	SKG	S1G	S2G	S3G	S4G[2]
PBI-Classroom Conduct	E>C	E>C*	E>C	E>C**	——
PBI-Socio-Emotional State	E=C	E>C	E>C**	E>C	——
PBI-Teacher Dependence	E<C	E>C	E=C	E>C	——
PBI-Personal Behavior	E<C	E>C**	E>C**	E>C	——
YRS-Social Development	E=C	E>C	E>C***	E>C*	——
YRS-Emotional Adjustment	E<C	E>C	E>C*	E>C*	——

[1]More complete results are presented in the *Statistical Supplement*, Part A, Tables 18a-26a.

[2]No data were collected on these measures during fourth grade.

*Asterisks indicate significance level (*p<.10; **p<.05; ***p<.01). If no asterisks appear, the difference is not significant at or beyond the .10 level.*

[24]Based on sign test (Hays, 1963; p. 625).

Figure 13

*Average PBI Classroom Conduct Factor Scores
for Experimental and Control Groups*

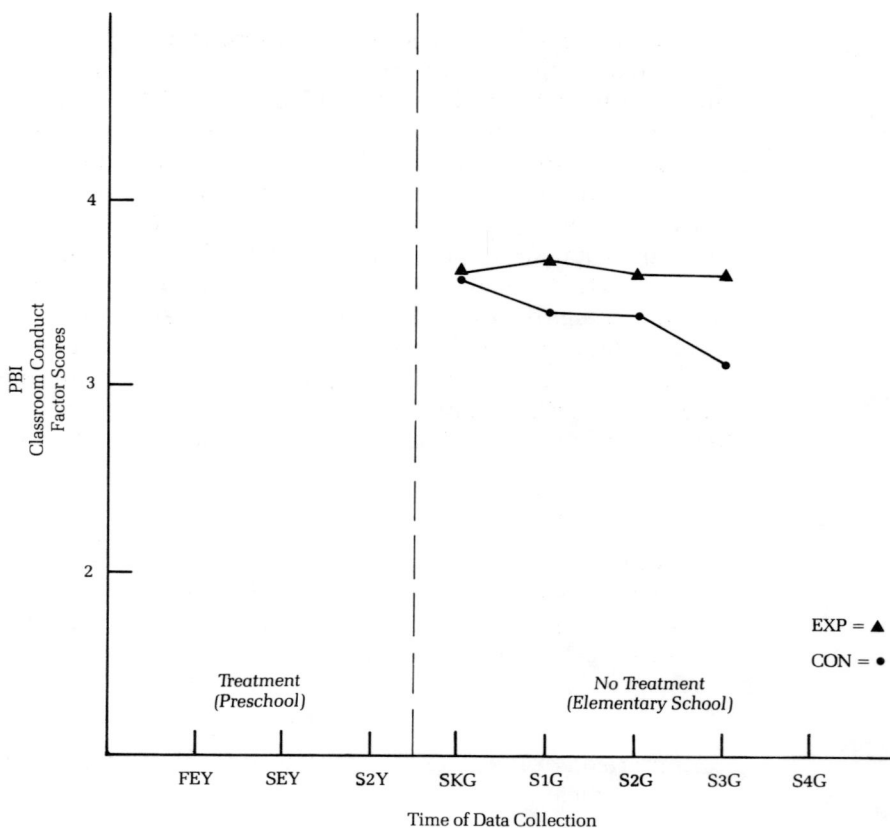

Arithmetic Means, Standard Deviations,
Number of Subjects, and Significance Levels of F Tests
on Group Comparisons at Each Testpoint

		Time of Data Collection							
		FEY	SEY	S2Y	SKG	S1G	S2G	S3G	S4G
EXP	Mean	——	——	——	3.60	3.66	3.60	3.59	——
	(S.D.)	——	——	——	(0.64)	(0.78)	(0.89)	(0.93)	——
	N	——	——	——	55	48	44	38	——
CON	Mean	——	——	——	3.56	3.39	3.37	3.11	——
	(S.D.)	——	——	——	(0.67)	(0.76)	(0.86)	(0.93)	——
	N	——	——	——	62	56	47	40	——
Significance of F Tests		——	——	——	N.S.	<.10	N.S.	<.05	——

F tests presented here were obtained in three-way analyses of variance (Group x Sex x Wave)
reported in the *Statistical Supplement*, Part A, Tables 21a-21c.

Figure 14

Average PBI Socio-Emotional Status Factor Scores
for Experimental and Control Groups

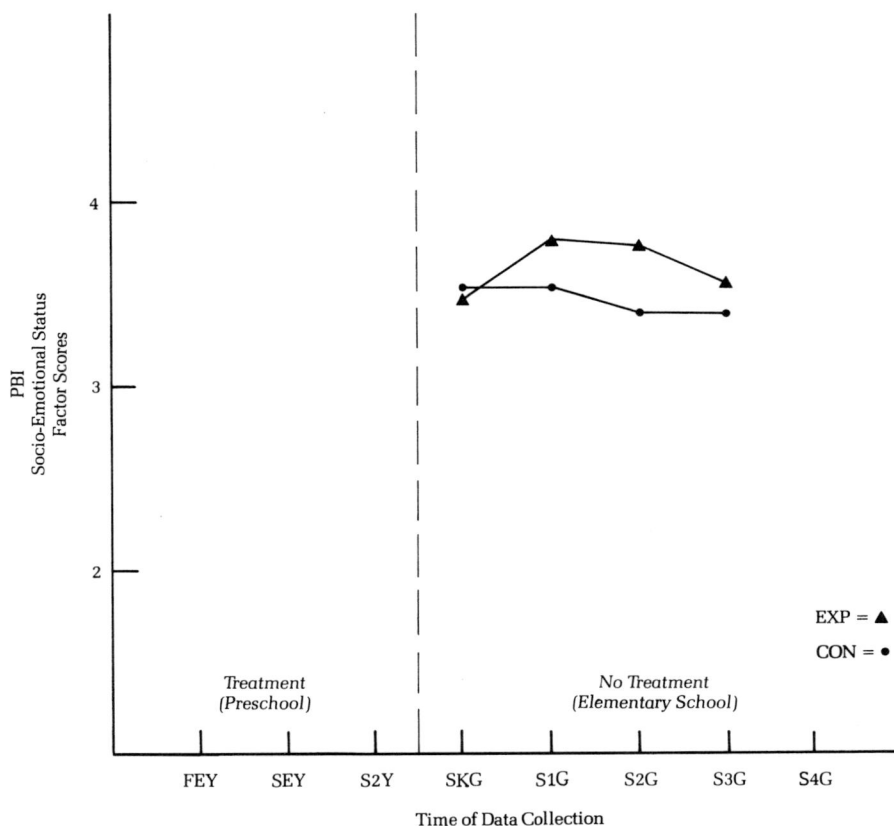

Arithmetic Means, Standard Deviations,
Number of Subjects, and Significance Levels of F Tests
on Group Comparisons at Each Testpoint

		Time of Data Collection							
		FEY	SEY	S2Y	SKG	S1G	S2G	S3G	S4G
EXP	Mean	——	——	——	3.46	3.78	3.75	3.54	——
	(S.D.)	——	——	——	(0.86)	(0.70)	(0.79)	(1.01)	——
	N	——	——	——	55	48	44	38	——
CON	Mean	——	——	——	3.51	3.52	3.39	3.39	——
	(S.D.)	——	——	——	(0.71)	(0.84)	(0.90)	(0.92)	——
	N	——	——	——	62	56	47	39	——
Significance of F Tests		——	——	——	N.S.	N.S.	<.05	N.S.	——

F tests presented here were obtained in three-way analyses of variance (Group x Sex x Wave)
reported in the *Statistical Supplement*, Part A, Tables 22a-22c.

Figure 15

*Average PBI Personal Behavior Factor Scores
for Experimental and Control Groups*

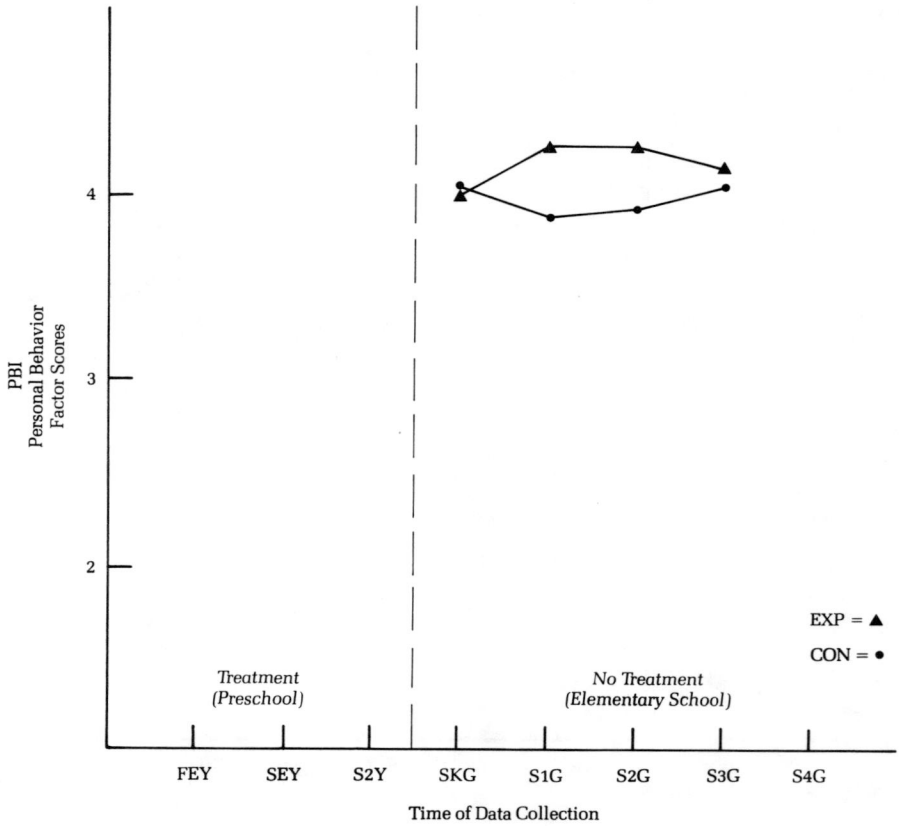

Arithmetic Means, Standard Deviations,
Number of Subjects, and Significance Levels of F Tests
on Group Comparisons at Each Testpoint

		Time of Data Collection							
		FEY	SEY	S2Y	SKG	S1G	S2G	S3G	S4G
EXP	Mean	——	——	——	3.99	4.25	4.25	4.13	——
	(S.D.)	——	——	——	(0.68)	(0.53)	(0.61)	(0.71)	——
	N	——	——	——	55	48	44	37	——
CON	Mean	——	——	——	4.03	3.87	3.91	4.03	——
	(S.D.)	——	——	——	(0.63)	(0.70)	(0.66)	(0.72)	——
	N	——	——	——	62	56	47	40	——
Significance of F Tests		——	——	——	N.S.	<.05	<.10	N.S.	——

F tests presented here were obtained in three-way analyses of variance (Group x Sex x Wave) reported in the *Statistical Supplement*, Part A, Tables 24a-24c.

Figure 16

Average PBI Teacher Dependence Factor Scores
for Experimental and Control Groups

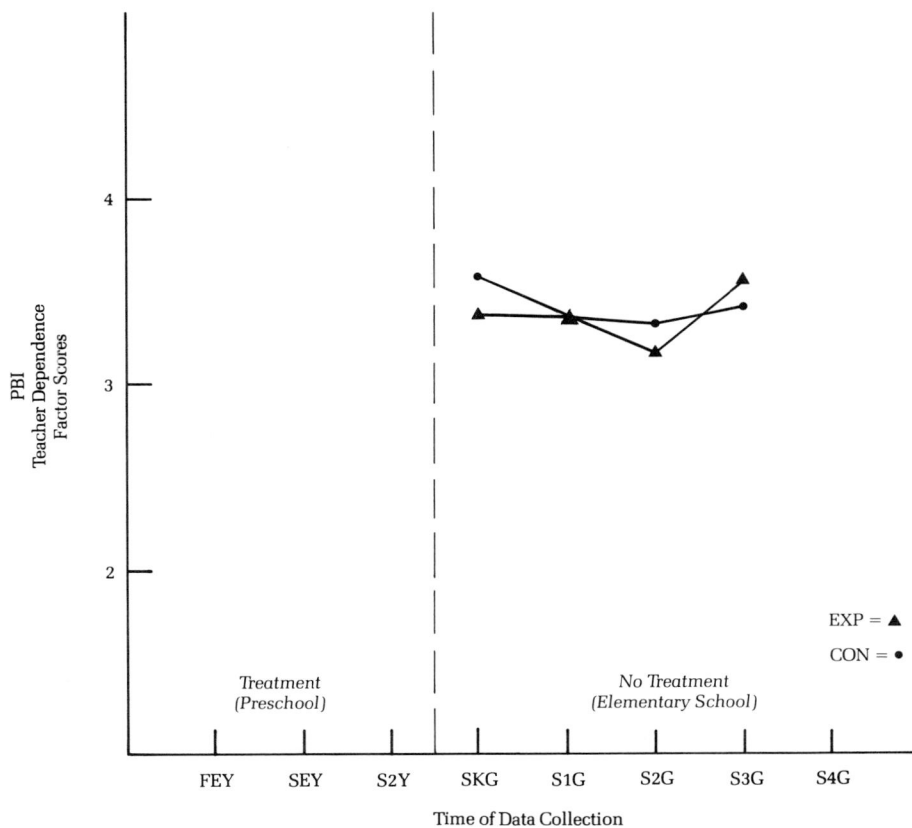

Arithmetic Means, Standard Deviations,
Number of Subjects, and Significance Levels of F Tests
on Group Comparisons at Each Testpoint

		Time of Data Collection							
		FEY	SEY	S2Y	SKG	S1G	S2G	S3G	S4G
EXP	Mean	——	——	——	3.36	3.35	3.26	3.55	——
	(S.D.)	——	——	——	(0.73)	(0.99)	(1.01)	(0.87)	——
	N	——	——	——	55	48	44	38	——
CON	Mean	——	——	——	3.57	3.35	3.32	3.41	——
	(S.D.)	——	——	——	(0.71)	(0.87)	(1.03)	(0.93)	——
	N	——	——	——	62	56	47	40	——
Significance of F Tests		——	——	——	N.S.	N.S.	N.S.	N.S.	——

F tests presented here were obtained in three-way analyses of variance (Group x Sex x Wave)
reported in the *Statistical Supplement*, Part A, Tables 23a-23c.

Figure 17

*Average YRS Social Development Factor Scores
for Experimental and Control Groups*

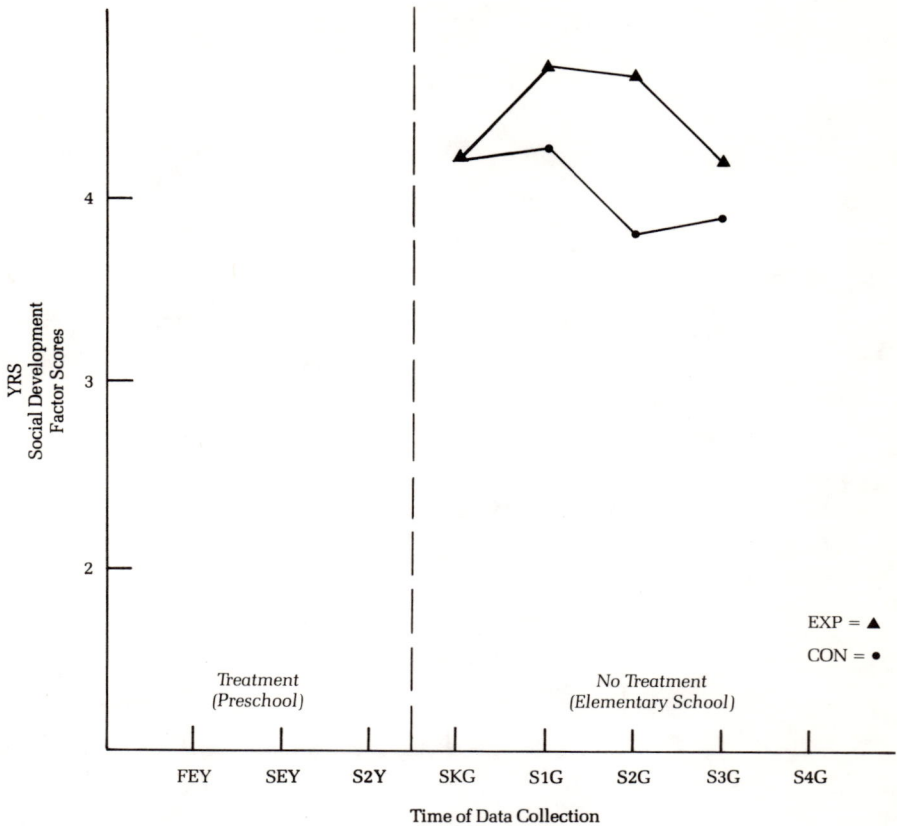

Arithmetic Means, Standard Deviations,
Number of Subjects, and Significance Levels of F Tests
on Group Comparisons at Each Testpoint

		Time of Data Collection							
		FEY	SEY	S2Y	SKG	S1G	S2G	S3G	S4G
EXP	Mean	——	——	——	4.28	4.70	4.64	4.26	——
	(S.D.)	——	——	——	(1.49)	(1.30)	(1.40)	(1.54)	——
	N	——	——	——	55	47	44	50	——
CON	Mean	——	——	——	4.28	4.35	3.79	3.87	——
	(S.D.)	——	——	——	(1.23)	(1.50)	(1.43)	(1.59)	——
	N	——	——	——	62	56	47	51	——
Significance of F Tests		——	——	——	N.S.	N.S.	<.01	<.10	——

F tests presented here were obtained in three-way analyses of variance (Group x Sex x Wave)
reported in the *Statistical Supplement*, Part A, Tables 25a-25c.

Figure 18

*Average YRS Emotional Adjustment Factor Scores
for Experimental and Control Groups*

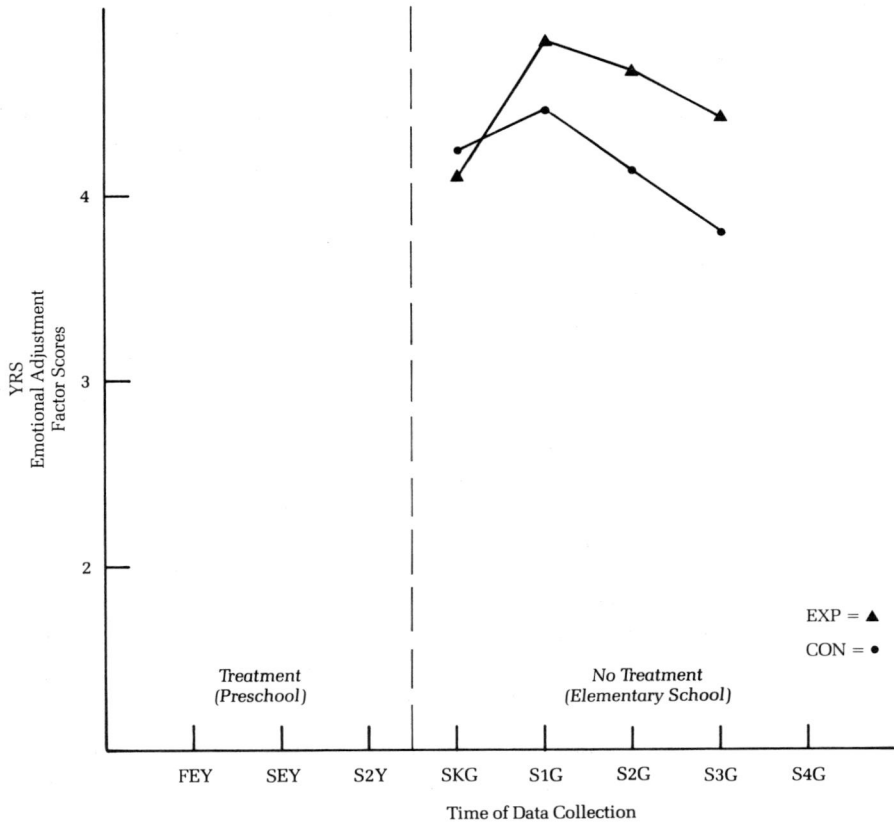

Arithmetic Means, Standard Deviations,
Number of Subjects, and Significance Levels of F Tests
on Group Comparisons at Each Testpoint

			Time of Data Collection						
		FEY	SEY	S2Y	SKG	S1G	S2G	S3G	S4G
EXP	Mean	——	——	——	4.10	4.83	4.66	4.41	——
	(S.D.)	——	——	——	(1.37)	(1.52)	(1.39)	(1.64)	——
	N	——	——	——	55	47	44	50	——
CON	Mean	——	——	——	4.23	4.46	4.12	3.80	——
	(S.D.)	——	——	——	(1.35)	(1.63)	(1.43)	(1.49)	——
	N	——	——	——	62	56	47	51	——
Significance of F Tests		——	——	——	N.S.	N.S.	<.10	<.10	——

F tests presented here were obtained in three-way analyses of variance (Group x Sex x Wave)
reported in the *Statistical Supplement*, Part A, Tables 26a-26c.

Findings

Children who attended preschool achieved significantly greater school success, that is, they were less likely to be retained in grade or placed in special education programs than control-group children.

Discussion

Question 1c was addressed using both conventional three-way analysis of variance (ANOVA) and multiple linear regression techniques. The results obtained using each method are presented separately below.

ANOVA results. Question 1c was first addressed using a conventional three-way analysis of variance design. The Group effect was tested with the effects of Sex, Wave, and all interactions of Group, Sex, and Wave statistically controlled. Although the experimental group was expected to achieve greater school success than the control group, the significance levels reported in Figure 19 are from nondirectional F tests, most commonly used in reporting ANOVA results.

Children who attended the experimental preschool were more successful (less often retained in grade or placed in special education) in elementary school than children from the control group (Figure 19). Differences between the two groups increased steadily during the post-treatment period, attaining statistical significance ($p<0.05$) at S3G and S4G. Treatment Group Membership accounted for about 4% of the variance in School Success scores at S3G and 4.5% at S4G. By fourth grade, 38% of control-group children, but only 17% of experimental-group children, had been retained in grade or placed in special education, a difference of 21%. When the distribution of children from the two groups across the three categories of School Success were examined, the findings were consistently in favor of the experimental group by S3G and S4G. Specifically, more experimental-group children than would have been expected by chance were on grade and in regular classrooms; and fewer than would have been expected by chance were retained in grade or placed in special education.

Although experimental-group children consistently performed at somewhat higher levels on standardized tests and tended to receive higher teacher ratings on scales of academic potential and socio-emotional maturity than children in the control group, differences between the two groups during the post-treatment period were rather small and not of obvious educational importance. This is to say, a program evaluation based on indicators of how well children were likely to do in school would have been inconclusive. *Data on actual school success through fourth grade, however, provide concrete evidence of the benefits which can derive from preschool, both to the child, insofar as he is better able to cope with the demands of school, and to the community, by way of reducing educational costs.*[25]

---

[25]See Weber, C. U., Foster, P. F., and Weikart, D. P. (1978) for an economic analysis of the social rate of return generated by the Perry Project.

Figure 19

Average School Success Scores
for Experimental and Control Groups

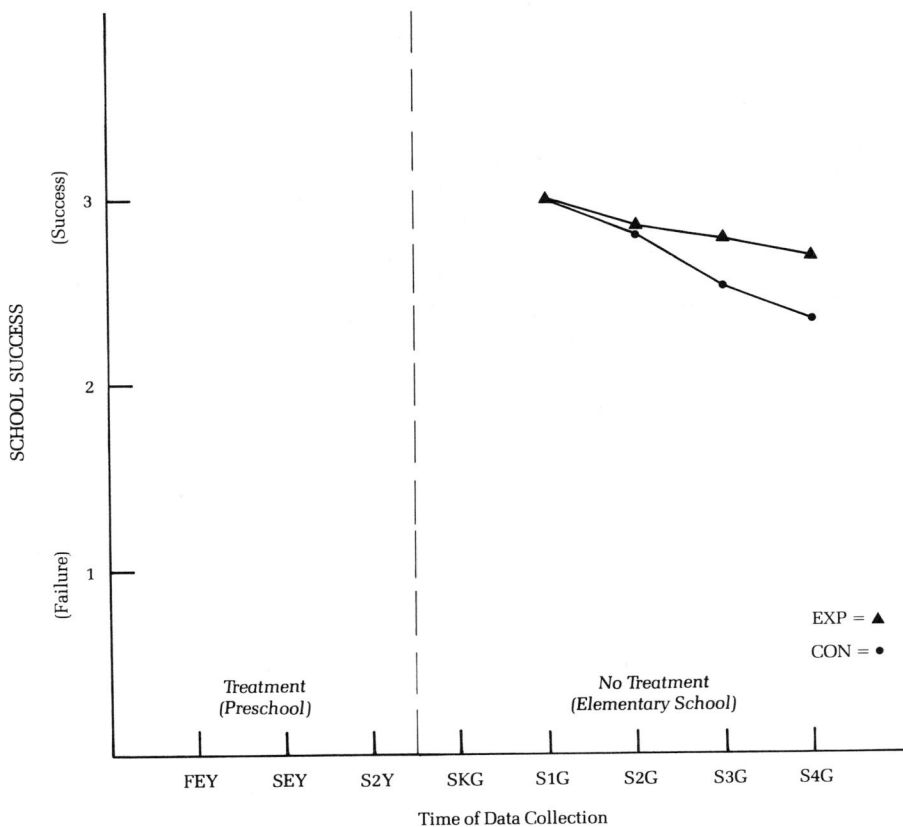

Time of Data Collection

Arithmetic Means, Standard Deviations,
Number of Subjects, and Significance Levels of F Tests
on Group Comparisons at Each Testpoint

		Time of Data Collection							
		FEY	SEY	S2Y	SKG	S1G	S2G	S3G	S4G
EXP	Mean	—	—	—	—	2.97	2.84	2.78	2.69
	(S.D.)	—	—	—	—	(0.18)	(0.49)	(0.62)	(0.71)
	N	—	—	—	—	58	58	58	58
CON	Mean	—	—	—	—	2.98	2.80	2.52	2.34
	(S.D.)	—	—	—	—	(0.12)	(0.54)	(0.81)	(0.89)
	N	—	—	—	—	65	65	65	65
Significance of F Tests		—	—	—	—	N.S.	N.S.	<.05	<.05

F tests presented here were obtained in three-way analyses of variance (Group x Sex x Wave) reported in the *Statistical Supplement*, Part A, Tables 30a-30c.

Regression results. The hypothesis that experimental-group children would be more successful in school than children in the control group was also tested using multiple linear regression techniques. School Success at S4G was predicted by Treatment Group Membership, covarying on Entering Child Characteristics and Home Environment Factors. Directional F tests were computed.

Group accounted for a significant amount of variance in actual school success, fewer children in the experimental than in the control group having been retained in grade or placed in special education programs as of fourth grade (Table 19). The magnitude of the Group effect (3%) is slightly less than that obtained in the three-way ANOVA already reported.

A supplemental regression analysis, incorporating mother's employment status at FEY as an additional covariate, was also performed. At project entry, 31% of control-group mothers but only 9% of experimental-group mothers were employed. Correlational analysis of the relationship between mother's employment status (1 = not employed; 2+ = employed) and School Success indicated that children of mothers who were working at FEY tended to be more successful in school than other children regardless of treatment. When mother's employment status at FEY was incorporated in regression equations as an additional predictor of S4G School Success, the magnitude of the Group effect increased from 3% to 5% (Table 19, bracketed proportion), which is comparable to the level obtained in the conventional analysis of variance already reported.

■ *Question 2:* **For the total sample, what was the relative influence of Treatment Group Membership, Entering Child Characteristics, and Home Environment Factors on Binet and CAT performance and School Success during the post-treatment period? (Analysis by multiple linear regression; each main effect was tested over and above the other two.)**

Findings

Entering Child Characteristics was by far the most important predictor of post-treatment Binet Performance, followed by Home Environment Factors and Treatment Group Membership (which had been the most important predictor during the preschool period). However, Home Environment Factors had more influence on CAT performance than either Treatment Group Membership or Entering Child Characteristics. Treatment Group Membership, Entering Child Characteristics, and Home Environment Factors had similar impacts on School Success.

Unlike the preschool period, in the post-treatment period Treatment Group Membership was not the most powerful of the three predictors of Binet scores (Table 17). Experimental-group children scored significantly higher than control-group children only during the first two years of elementary school, Group explaining 4% (p<.01) of the variance in Binet scores at SKG, 3% (p<.05) at S1G, and less than 1% thereafter. The most powerful predictor of Binet scores for the total sample throughout the

Table 19

Main Effects of Treatment Group Membership, Entering Child Characteristics, and Home Environment Factors upon Fourth-Grade School Success

CRITERION MEASURES	SAMPLE SIZE N	Proportion of Variance in Criterion Measures Explained by Full Regression Model R^2_f	PREDICTORS				
			Treatment Group[1]		Child Characteristics[2]	Environmental Factors[2]
			Magnitude of Effect Over and Above Other Predictors $R^2_f - R^2_T(a)$	Direction of Difference E/C	Magnitude of Effect Over and Above Other Predictors $R^2_f - R^2_T(b)$	Magnitude of Effect Over and Above Other Predictors $R^2_f - R^2_T(c)$
S4G SCHOOL SUCCESS	98	.25	.03**[.05***][3]	E > C	.09**	.07

[1] A directional F test was used to determine the statistical significance of the Group Effect.

[2] Nondirectional F tests were used to determine the statistical significance of the effects of Child Characteristics and Environmental Factors.

[3] The proportions reported in brackets represent the magnitude of the Group main effect when one additional covariate—mother's employment status—was incorporated in the regression design. See text for discussion.

Asterisks indicate significance level (*p<.10; **p<.05; ***p<.01). If no asterisks appear, the difference is not significant at or beyond the .10 level.

post-treatment period was Entering Child Characteristics (the joint effect of FEY Binet, FEY Leiter/R, FEY ITPA/R, and FEY PPVT/R), which accounted for 12-13% of the variance in Binet scores at SKG through S4G (p<.01 at SKG-S3G; p<.05 at S4G). Home Environment Factors (the joint effect of Mother's Education, SES, CHES1/R, CHES2/R, and MAI/R) were more important predictors than Group during the post-treatment period but far less important on the whole than Entering Child Characteristics. Home Environment Factors accounted for 6% to 9% of the variance in Binet scores (p<.01 at S1G, S3G, and S4G; N.S. at SKG and S2G). Neither Entering Child Characteristics nor Home Environment Factors unambiguously declined or increased in predictive power over time. Between 10% and 15% of the variance in Binet scores explained by the joint effect of the predictor variables (full regression model) from SKG through S4G could not be uniquely attributed to individual predictors. The magnitude of the joint effect (R^2) of Group, Entering Child Characteristics, and Home Environment Factors on Binet performance during the post-treatment period was comparable to that found during the preschool period and surprisingly large considering the intervals over which predictions were made (3 through 7 years).

There was a persistently significant, albeit rather small, treatment-group effect at all testpoints on CAT scores (Table 17). The importance of Entering Child Characteristics versus Home Environment Factors was the reverse of the pattern observed in predictions of post-treatment-period Binet scores. Although Entering Child Characteristics explained 15% (p<.01) of the variance in CAT scores at S1G, the effects of this predictor were small and not significant from S2G through S4G. Home Environment Factors, however, were consistently strong and significant (p<.01) predictors of CAT scores for the total sample throughout the post-treatment period, explaining 15% through 19% of the variance in the criterion. Again, the magnitude of the joint effect (R^2) of the three sets of predictor variables is quite large considering the interval over which predictions were made. Between 10% and 14% of the variance in CAT scores explained by the joint effect of the predictors could not be uniquely attributed to individual predictors.

Both Group and Entering Child Characteristics predicted small but significant proportions of variance in School Success at S4G. The proportion of variance in the criterion explained by Home Environment Factors was of similar magnitude but did not quite reach statistical significance (p<.10) in a nondirectional F test. Comparing relative magnitudes of effects rather than significance levels, it can be seen that Group, Entering Child Characteristics, and Home Environment Factors had quite similar impacts upon School Success. Although the amount of variance explained by the joint effect (R^2) of the three predictors seems small (25%) when compared with that explained in predictions of Binet and CAT scores, it increased substantially when interactions were included (from 25% to 40%; Table 20).

- *Question 3:* **Did boys and girls in the experimental group benefit differentially from the experimental treatment? (Analysis by conventional analysis of variance; the Group x Sex interaction was tested**

Table 20

Effects of Interactions of Treatment Group Membership with Entering Child Characteristics and Home Environment Factors upon Criterion Measures Obtained during the Post-Treatment Period

CRITERION MEASURES	SAMPLE SIZE N	Proportion of Variance in Criterion Measures Explained by Full Regression Model R^2_f	PREDICTORS			
			Group x Child Characteristics		Group x Environmental Factors	
			Magnitude of Effect Over and Above the Group x Environmental Factors Interaction $R^2_f - R^2_{f(d)}$	Relative Magnitude of Effects Across Groups[1] E/C	Magnitude of Effect Over and Above the Group x Child Characteristics Interaction $R^2_f - R^2_{f(e)}$	Relative Magnitude of Effects Across Groups[1] E/C
SKG BINET	98	.50	.06*	E > C	.03	—
S1G BINET	95	.42	.02	—	.02	—
S2G BINET	93	.46	.14***	E > C	.01	—
S3G BINET	92	.48	.01	—	.03	—
S4G BINET	92	.33	.00	—	.02	—
S1G CAT-TOTAL	90	.51	.04	—	.04	—
S2G CAT-TOTAL	85	.46	.01	—	.08*	C > E
S3G CAT-TOTAL	86	.44	.02	—	.08*	C > E
S4G CAT-TOTAL	76	.43	.02	—	.05	—
S4G SCHOOL SUCCESS	98	.40	.06	—	.08**	C > E

[1]The relative magnitude of effects across groups is reported only when interactions reach significance at the .10 level or better. A nondirectional F test was used to determine the statistical significance of the Group x Entering Child Characteristics interaction; a directional F test, to determine the significance of the Group x Home Environment Factors interaction (see text).

Asterisks indicate significance level (*p<.10; **p<.05; ***p<.01). If no asterisks appear, the difference is not significant at or beyond the .10 level.

with the effects of Group, Sex, and Wave and the Group x Wave, Sex x Wave, and Group x Sex x Wave interactions statistically controlled.)

Findings

No consistently significant Sex differences on post-treatment-period outcome measures were found in either treatment group.

Discussion

A series of planned comparisons (Hays, 1963) was carried out to test a hypothesis generated by the 1970 Perry Report. Findings presented in the previous report suggested that girls benefited more than boys from the experimental treatment as judged by CAT performance. For this report, the simple effect (Winer, 1962) of Sex within treatment group was tested using two orthogonal comparisons of Group x Sex means on CAT subtests and total scores at each testpoint from S1G through S4G.[26] Specifically, it was hypothesized that girls would score significantly higher on CAT tests than boys in the experimental group but not in the control group. One-tailed t tests were used to evaluate comparisons within the experimental group where the direction of difference was hypothesized (girls>boys). Two-tailed tests were used for the control-group comparisons where no difference was anticipated. No significant Sex effect was found within the control group at any testpoint. Although girls scored consistently higher than boys in the experimental group, the only significant (p<.05) differences appeared on the Reading subtest at S1G and S2G and the total score at S2G. Thus, while there was some indication that experimental girls had better reading skills than experimental boys in first and second grades, no consistently significant Sex difference in overall achievement test performance was found. For the sake of convenience,[27] the Group x Sex interaction term was included in analyses of variance of CAT data as though no planned comparisons had been performed.

When all Group x Sex interactions from analyses of post-treatment-period data are considered (see the *Statistical Supplement*, Part A), no consistent pattern of differences emerges, and the number of significant (p<.10 or better) interactions does not exceed chance levels. Interestingly, no Group x Sex interactions in CAT subtest or total scores reached significance (*Statistical Supplement*, Part A, Tables 14b-17b). Since any strong simple effect of Sex within group would have appeared as a significant interaction, it seems legitimate to conclude that no replicable simple effects were present.

---

[26]The use of planned comparisons in this situation was not entirely justified since part of the data analyzed in this report coincides with data analyzed in the previous report, from which the hypothesis being tested was derived. Consequently, the Type I error rate is somewhat inflated.

[27]Available computer programs for performing three-way ANOVA's did not permit collapsing this interaction into the error term.

■ *Question 4:* **Did experimental-group children in different waves (replication samples) benefit differentially from preschool? (Analysis by conventional analysis of variance; the Group x Wave interaction was tested with the effects of Group, Sex, and Wave and Group x Sex, Sex x Wave, and Group x Sex x Wave interactions statistically controlled.)**

Findings

Evolution of the preschool program from year to year does not seem to have had systematic effects on the test performance, teacher ratings, or school success of children in the experimental group.

Discussion

Consistently significant ($p<.10$ or better) Group x Wave interactions appeared only on CAT Language subtests (see the *Statistical Supplement*, Part A, Table 17b). Although the pattern of differences was not perfectly consistent across testpoints, Waves 0 and 2 tended to score somewhat higher than other waves in the experimental group, and Wave 4 scored higher than other waves in the control group.[28] When all significant ($p<.10$) interactions (20 out of 109 possible) are examined for the post-treatment period, a similar pattern emerges (*Statistical Supplement*, Part A, Tables 1b-26b, and 30b).

Although the pattern of wave differences within treatment groups for significant interactions suggests that successive experimental waves may have benefited less from preschool, visual inspection of all Group x Wave means in the *Statistical Supplement*, Part A contradicts this impression. Significant (often marginally significant) interactions were not necessarily those most representative of the overall pattern within the experimental group and seem to have been as much a result of wave differences in the "untreated" control group as of differences in the experimental group potentially related to changes in the preschool program across waves. For example, since Wave 4 control-group children tended to score higher than other children in the control group and on a par with children in the experimental group on all measures, relatively poor performance by Wave 4 experimental-group children at a particular testpoint tended to produce a significant interaction, suggesting that while performance increased with succeeding waves in the control group, it decreased in the experimental group. This phenomenon is clearly illustrated in the case of CAT Language subtest scores. Yet, the overall pattern of wave effects within the experimental group indicates that experimental Wave 4 was one of the most successful experimental waves (along with Waves 0 and 2) in spite of the fact that they occasionally scored lower than the Wave 4 control group and other experimental waves.

Limited explorations of the simple effects of Wave within the experi-

---

[28]It is possible that Wave 4 control-group children experienced the impact of federally funded Title I programs which were initiated at about the time they entered kindergarten.

mental group utilizing techniques for *post hoc* comparisons indicated that no parsimonious explanation was possible. In short, the pattern of differences in wave means within the experimental group was not sufficiently systematic or pronounced to suggest that changes in the preschool program associated with waves had a significant effect on test performance, teacher ratings, or success in school.

> ■ *Question 5:* Did Entering Child Characteristics have different effects on Binet and CAT elementary-school test performance and School Success *within* the experimental and control groups? (Analysis by multiple linear regression; the interaction of Group with Entering Child Characteristics was tested over and above the effects of Group, Home Environment Factors, Entering Child Characteristics, and the interaction of Group with Home Environment Factors.)

Findings

The only indication that Entering Child Characteristics had significantly different effects on post-treatment-period outcomes in the experimental and control groups was found in predictions of Binet performance where entering level of academic potential (Entering Child Characteristics) tended to influence Binet performance more in the experimental than control group at SKG and S2G.

Discussion

The interaction between Treatment Group Membership and Entering Child Characteristics had significant effects on Binet scores at SKG ($p<.10$) and S2G ($p<.01$), the magnitude of effect being greatest in the experimental group (Table 20). Although these findings suggest that Entering Child Characteristics—measures of academic potential—may be better predictors of later Binet performance among children who have attended preschool than among children who have not, the interaction effect was neither consistently significant nor in the same direction over all testpoints. In fact, at the three testpoints (S1G, S3G, and S4G) where significant effects were not found, Entering Child Characteristics were slightly better predictors of Binet scores in the control group than in the experimental group.

The interaction between Group and Entering Child Characteristics did not explain significant amounts of variance in either CAT scores or School Success, indicating that the effects of entering level of academic potential were the same in both the experimental and the control group.

> ■ *Question 6:* Did Home Environment Factors have different effects on elementary-school test performance (Binet and CAT) and School Success *within* the experimental and control groups? (Analysis by multiple linear regression; the interaction of Group with Home Environment Factors was tested over and above the effects of Group,

Home Environment Factors, Entering Child Characteristics, and the interaction of Entering Child Characteristics with Group.)

Findings

Home Environment Factors seem to have had the same effects on Binet performance in both treatment groups. However, they were more powerful predictors of CAT scores and School Success in the control than in the experimental group. This finding supports expectations that the preschool experience with home teaching would tend to compensate for environmental differences which normally influence academic achievement.

Discussion

The hypothesis that Home Environment Factors would have more influence on child outcomes in the control than in the experimental group was evaluated by directional F tests. The interaction of Group with Home Environment Factors did not account for significant amounts of variance in Binet performance, indicating that the effects of Home Environment Factors were the same in both groups. However, the Group x Home Environment Factors interaction *did* predict CAT scores ($p < .10$) at S2G and S3G and School Success ($p < .05$), explaining 8% of the variance in each of these criterion measures (Table 20). Although the interaction effect was not consistently significant across all CAT testpoints, the simple effect of Home Environment Factors was greatest within the control group on all CATs and the School Success variable.

In sum, the preschool experience of experimental-group children seems to have reduced the effects of home environment not only upon the acquisition of academic skills (suggested by findings presented in the 1970 Perry Report) but upon actual success in school as well.

■ *Question 7:* **Were outcomes different for boys and girls in the total sample on aptitude and achievement measures, on teacher ratings of socio-emotional development, and in actual school success? (Analysis by conventional analysis of variance; the Sex main effect was tested with the effects of Group, Wave, and all interactions of Group, Sex, and Wave statistically controlled.)**

Findings

Although the direction of differences in mean scores for boys and girls was fairly consistent for a number of measures, the only consistently significant comparisons appeared (1) on the ITPA-AVAS and PPVT tests after SKG, and ITPA-Total after S1G, favoring boys over girls and (2) on teachers' ratings of Classroom Conduct (PBI) from SKG through S2G, favoring girls over boys.

Discussion

The pattern of sex differences on aptitude indices is rather striking (Table 21a). On measures of general cognitive and linguistic ability (Binet, Leiter, PPVT, ITPA-Total and ITPA-AVAS subtest) boys scored consistently higher than girls during the post-treatment period, with the exception of Binet tests at SKG and S1G. Boys scored significantly higher ($p < .10$ or better) than girls on the PPVT and the ITPA-AVAS subtest from first grade through the final administration of these tests at S3G, and significantly higher on the ITPA-Total at S2G and S3G. On measures of specific academic skills (CAT), however, girls scored higher than boys, with the exception of the CAT Arithmetic subtest for which results were mixed. The only significant sex differences in CAT scores appeared on the CAT-Total and Language subtest at S2G. Although teacher ratings of academic potential did not consistently differentiate girls from boys dur-

Table 21

*Comparison of Sex Means for the Post-Treatment Period
Indicating Results of F Tests from Analyses of Variance*

ELEMENTARY SCHOOL MEASURES	CURRENT FINDINGS				
	SKG	S1G	S2G	S3G	S4G
A. Indices of Academic Potential					
BINET	B<G	B<G	B>G	B>G	B>G
LEITER	B>G	B>G	B>G	B>G	——
PPVT	B>G	B>G**	B>G*	B>G***	——
ITPA-TOTAL	B>G	B>G	B>G**	B>G***	——
ITPA-AVAS	B>G	B>G**	B>G***	B>G**	——
CAT-TOTAL	——	B<G	B<G*	B<G	B<G
CAT-Reading	——	B<G	B<G	B<G	B<G
CAT-Arithmetic	——	B>G	B<G	B<G	B>G
CAT-Language	——	B<G	B<G**	B<G	B<G
PBI-Academic Motivation	B<G	B<G	B<G	B=G	——
YRS-Academic Potential	B>G	B<G	B<G**	B>G	——
YRS-Verbal Skill	B>G	B>G	B<G	B<G	——
B. Measures of Socio-Emotional Development					
PBI-Classroom Conduct	B<G***	B<G*	B<G*	B<G	——
PBI-Socio-Emotional State	B>G	B>G	B<G**	B>G	——
PBI-Teacher Dependence	B<G	B>G	B>G	B>G	——
PBI-Personal Behavior	B<G	B<G*	B<G**	B=G	——
YRS-Social Development	B=G	B>G	B<G	B>G	——
YRS-Emotional Adjustment	B=G	B<G	B<G	B<G	——
C. Measures of School Success					
School Success	——	B>G	B>G	B>G	B>G

More complete results are presented in the *Statistical Supplement*, Part A, Tables 1a-4a, 8a, 14a-26a.

Asterisks indicate significance level (*p<.10; **p<.05; ***p<.01). If no asterisks appear, the difference is not significant at or beyond the .10 level.

ing the elementary school years, the only significant (p<.05) difference on these measures favored girls over boys (YRS-AP at S2G).

Teachers rated girls as having more acceptable Classroom Conduct (PBI) and Personal Behavior (PBI) than boys (Table 21b). Significant (p<.10) differences favoring girls over boys appeared at SKG through S2G on the Personal Behavior scale. Girls were also rated higher in Emotional Adjustment (YRS) than boys after SKG, though no significant differences were found. On only one socio-emotional scale did boys tend to be rated higher than girls: boys were judged to exhibit slightly less Teacher Dependence (PBI) than girls from first through third grades. These differences, however, were not significant.

Sex means on the School Success measure consistently, albeit insignificantly, favored boys over girls (Table 21c). The absence of any significant sex difference in actual success in school strongly suggests that the relatively small differences between boys and girls on other measures were educationally unimportant. Yet, the pattern of results on measures of specific academic skills (CAT) and ratings of the social acceptability of children's classroom behavior (PBI-CC and PBI-PB) lends tentative support to the widely held opinion that girls are somewhat better adapted than boys to the demands of school and are more liked by teachers. Whether girls are better liked because they are better adapted or more readily adapt because they are more liked remains an unanswered question.

III Preschool's impact on children: conclusions and implications

The Perry Preschool Project provides an unusual opportunity to study the immediate and lasting impacts that preschool can have upon economically disadvantaged children. This chapter summarizes the major findings of the study, examines them in relation to the results of other compensatory preschool experiments, and explores the implications of the Perry Preschool Project and similar projects for early childhood education policy.

Impact on academic aptitude

Preschool attendance had an immediate and positive impact on the measured aptitude of children in the Perry Project sample. Large and highly significant differences were found between the experimental and control groups on all measures of aptitude—Binet, Leiter, PPVT, and ITPA—throughout the preschool period. Treatment group membership explained up to 33% of the variance in aptitude test scores during preschool. By the end of the treatment period, the experimental group had gained 15.3 points in Stanford-Binet IQ, scoring over 11 points higher than the control group. These and later differences cannot be explained away by "regression toward the mean", "test practice", or other threats to internal validity since the control group was equally subject to these effects.

After treatment terminated and all children entered elementary school, the magnitude of aptitude differences between the two groups diminished. Although children in the experimental group consistently scored somewhat higher than control-group children on all aptitude measures through fourth grade, these differences did not generally reach statistical significance. Significant differences on the Binet disappeared after first grade; PPVT differences disappeared after kindergarten. Although no significant differences appeared in Leiter or ITPA-Total scores from kindergarten through second grade, the experimental group unexpectedly scored significantly higher than the control group on both measures in third grade, the last point at which these instruments were administered. On rating scales of academic aptitude (YRS-AP, YRS-VS, and PBI-AM), elementary teachers consistently rated experimental-group children somewhat higher than control-group children; however, mean differences reached statistical significance at only one grade (second) on one of the three rating scales (YRS-VS). The only exception to this pattern of markedly attenuated post-treatment differences appeared in ITPA-Verbal Analogy subtest scores, where the experimental group performed at significantly higher levels than the control group at all but one (spring second grade) data collection point.

Relation of Perry Project to other studies

The aptitude test results obtained in the Perry Preschool Project are not unique. A number of important compensatory preschool studies have reported treatment effects of similar magnitude during the period of intervention itself (e.g., Gray and Klaus, 1970; Karnes, 1973; Weikart, Epstein, Schweinhart, and Bond, 1978). However, it is also true that most preschool experiments have not produced such dramatic effects on aptitude test performance. For example, in Planned Variation Head Start, with the exception of High/Scope's Cognitively Oriented Curriculum program (derived from the Perry Project), Binet gains were small or nonexistent (Smith, 1973). Small or zero Binet IQ gains are also reported by Di Lorenzo et al. (1969) for a large number of community-organized preschool interventions in New York State and by Miller and Dyer (1975) for various model programs implemented by the Louisville, Kentucky school system. In short, strong concurrent effects of preschool upon IQ are unusual, though not unique.

The gradual attenuation of aptitude-test gains following preschool intervention in the Perry Project parallel the findings from most other compensatory preschool studies. The erosion of preschool effects once children enter regular public school is now a familiar pattern in the annals of education evaluation. Two apparent exceptions to this pattern of vanishing IQ gains, however, are reported in the literature and should be mentioned. Karnes (1973) reports that three programs in her study maintained some small part (about 6 points) of their initial IQ gains through third grade. Weikart et al. (1978) report that the three programs compared in the Ypsilanti Curriculum Demonstration (CD) Project maintained about 15 points of their initial IQ gains through fourth grade. The results of the latter project are particularly pertinent to the study reported here. The preschool models compared included High/Scope's Cognitively Oriented Curriculum (developed in the Perry Project) as well as a traditional "unit-based" program and a Bereiter-Engelmann language program; all three programs effected long-term changes in children's Binet IQ of considerable magnitude. Why children in the Cognitively Oriented Curriculum program in this project maintained their initial IQ gains while children from the experimental group of the Perry Preschool Project did not is unclear; however, various program differences may be responsible. Differences in the children served by the two projects, improvements in the curriculum during the Curriculum Demonstration Project, modifications in the program delivery system, and/or changes in local public-school education may have been responsible.

Binet performance in the control group

The pattern of Binet performance in the control group merits consideration in its own right. Since children in the Perry Project sample were selected specifically because of their low SES and low Binet IQ, it was anticipated that children's Binet scores would increase somewhat—"regressing toward the population mean"—upon second testing, regardless of treatment.[29] The change in Binet IQ of the control group from initial to second testing at the end of the first project year was +4.8 points.

[29]The "true" scores of children selected for their extremely low scores relative to the population being sampled will, in general, be higher than the scores that they actually obtained and by which they were selected, assuming that the measure is not perfectly

This gain is our best estimate of "regression toward the mean" in Binet IQ for children in the Perry Project sample. It seems unlikely that testing procedures or acclimation to the test situation accounts for this gain since procedures were unchanging and closely resembled Zigler and Butterfield's (1968) "optimizing" conditions. Although a "practice effect" might be confounded with regression toward the mean, this too seems improbable given the nature of the test and the length of time between test administrations. Assuming that the regression effect was of the same magnitude in the experimental group, then perhaps only 10.5 points of the experimental group's 15.3 point gain in Binet IQ over two years of preschool represents the impact of treatment. This estimated "true" gain is approximately equal to the actual difference in mean Binet IQ between experimental and control groups measured at the end of preschool.

The upward inflection in the control group's Binet performance curve upon enrollment in kindergarten also deserves comment. On the average, children in the control group gained 2.8 points in Binet IQ during kindergarten and another point during first grade. It seems likely that gains of this magnitude might be expected for any group of economically disadvantaged children confronting a new and challenging educational experience. By the end of fourth grade, however, this school-related effect was no longer evident, and the control group's Binet performance had dropped to the level attained at second testing.

Measured aptitude at eighth grade

Preliminary analyses of WISC (Wechsler Intelligence Scale for Children) full-scale IQ scores obtained on all children at eighth grade confirm the finding of no difference in measured aptitude obtained at fourth grade. By this point, the performance of both experimental and control children was indistinguishable from entry-level performance on the Binet. These data are examined more completely in a recent article (Schweinhart and Weikart, 1977).

Impact on academic achievement

While differences in measured aptitude gradually diminished during the post-treatment period, differences in academic achievement between the experimental and control groups actually increased over time as measured by the California Achievement Test (CAT). Not only did the consistency of significant differences on CAT subtests increase from first through fourth grades, but the magnitude of the treatment effect grew steadily (this is particularly evident in the regression results presented in Table 17). Since the CAT specifically taps academic skills, these findings suggest that the preschool experience prepared experimental-group children to cope more effectively with school. To conclude that

reliable. Upon retesting, their scores will typically increase somewhat, regressing toward the population mean and more closely approximating their own "true" scores.

experimental-group children were better able to cope with elementary school as a result of preschool is not to suggest that they flourished in that environment: the achievement levels of both experimental and control children were in general well below community, not to mention national, norms. Nevertheless, achievement test differences favoring the experimental group represent long-term benefits of preschool that hold up in typical school settings which are certainly less than "the best of all possible worlds".

Relationship to other studies

There is little in the early childhood education literature to parallel this finding of achievement differences not merely persisting but growing through fourth grade. The majority of compensatory preschool studies with longitudinal follow-up report the attenuation or disappearance of achievement differences as time passes (e.g., Gray and Klaus, 1970; Kellaghan, 1977; Smith and James, 1975). Apparent exceptions to this pattern are reported by Palmer (1976) on a subgroup of his original sample, who obtained higher achievement test scores in fifth grade than children in the control group, and by Seitz, Apfel, and Efron (1976) for a sample of children who attended one of the national Follow Through programs after preschool, then obtained somewhat higher achievement test scores than a roughly matched comparison group at eighth grade. There are, however, no strong precedents for the findings obtained in the Perry Project.

Academic achievement at eighth grade

Preliminary analyses of achievement test data obtained at eighth grade, nine years after the preschool intervention, indicate that *the difference between the experimental and control groups continued to increase.* In eighth grade, the experimental group outperformed the control group on the CAT total score and on all but one subtest. The magnitude of the treatment effect was at least twice that found at fourth grade. Although achievement levels in the experimental group remain, in general, far below that of the national norm (as does achievement for the community as a whole), achievement gains by eighth grade would seem to be educationally as well as statistically significant.

Why an achievement difference?

The finding of a growing difference in achievement test performance favoring the experimental group was not anticipated; neither is it readily explained. To conclude that it was a "latent" or "sleeper effect" of the preschool treatment would seem to beg the question; however, thorough explanation would require far more information than is available. It seems likely that the observed divergence in achievement is the product of many "causes" in a multivariate chain linking the original treatment to later test performance. Perhaps small but persistent treatment effects evident in some measures of academic aptitude represented real differences in children's ability to cope with the academic demands of school, to acquire those basic skills measured by achievement tests. Perhaps the home teaching program had subtle effects upon parental attitudes and behavior, creating home environments more supportive of school-related learning. Perhaps differences between the experimental and control groups in grade retention and special education placement provided different opportunities to learn those things that achievement tests test. This latter possibility will be examined further in a subsequent section of this chapter.

Impact on social-emotional adjustment in school

The overall pattern of differences in teacher ratings (PBI-CC, PBI-SES, PBI-TD, PBI-PB, YRS-SD, YRS-EA) of children's social-emotional maturity consistently and significantly favored the experimental group after kindergarten. Comparisons at specific testpoints reached significance about a third of the time from kindergarten through fourth grade and one-half of the time in third and fourth grades. There was a general tendency for the magnitude of the treatment effect to increase over time. The absence of any significant differences at kindergarten suggests that experimental-group children had some difficulty adjusting to traditional kindergarten programs that were substantially more teacher-controlled and narrowly didactic than the Perry Preschool. Increasingly positive teacher assessments after kindergarten, however, indicate that experimental-group children more effectively adjusted their classroom behavior to fit the expectations of elementary teachers than control-group children. The experimental group's somewhat higher aptitude and academic skill may also have influenced teachers' assessments of their social-emotional adjustment.

Impact on actual school success

Most significantly, experimental-group children were found to be more successful in school as evaluated by the schools' own criteria of success. Actual school success was measured unobtrusively by ascertaining whether children were on grade in regular classrooms, retained in grade, or placed in special education programs in first through fourth grades. This measure was particularly meaningful for children in the Perry Project sample given the predicted high rates of retention and special education placement which were the impetus for the project in the first place.

No significant differences between experimental and control groups appeared in first or second grades, and few children from either group were retained or placed in special education. By third grade, however, significantly more children in the experimental group were on grade and in regular classrooms (88% in the experimental group versus 72% in the control group). The magnitude of this difference continued to increase such that 83% of experimental-group children, but only 62% of the control-group children, were on grade in regular classrooms by the end of fourth grade.

Findings of difference favoring the experimental group on standardized achievement measures and teacher ratings of social-emotional adjustment five years or more after preschool are impressive. Although programs in early childhood education are typically evaluated on the basis of such indicators, more direct measures of school success are desirable in a world of imperfect correlations. The measure of school success employed in this study is such an index, and it provides persuasive evidence of the benefits which can derive from preschool both for the child and for society at large.

What accounts for school success?

Differences in actual school success indicate that children in the experimental and control groups were perceived and treated differently by school personnel. Although decisions to retain children or to place them in special education programs may not be entirely objective, neither are they whimsical. The observations made by school personnel and their judgments of children's competence in kindergarten through second grade must account for the differential placement of experimental and control children beginning in third grade. Test results indicate that children in the experimental group exhibited somewhat greater academic aptitude and achievement during their first three years in school. However, since even experimental-group children tended to fall well below community norms, their slight edge over the control group in measured aptitude and achievement was probably insufficient by itself to account for observed differences in school success. Firsthand knowledge of the local school system suggests that grade retention and special education placement were importantly, perhaps most importantly, influenced by judgments of children's classroom behavior. The child with whom a teacher could not cope was a most likely candidate for failure in school, particularly if the child was unredeemed by high achievement. Consequently, teachers' judgments that experimental-group children were on the whole better adjusted, together with evidence of a somewhat higher level of academic skill, may well have contributed importantly to placement decisions.

It should also be noted that as a consequence of higher rates of retention in grade and assignment to special education programs emphasizing remedial instruction in rudimentary skills, more control-group children may have been deprived of experiences necessary to learning the higher-order reasoning skills tapped by achievement tests. Furthermore, their motivation to achieve and confidence in their own capacity to succeed in school may have been shaken by the experience of being singled out as academic failures.

Even among children who were not retained in grade or assigned to special education programs, however, the experimental group outperformed the control group on standardized achievement tests by eighth grade (based on preliminary analyses of data through eighth grade). This finding would seem to indicate that experimental-group children not only behaved more appropriately in the classroom and more often avoided retention in grade and placement in special education *but* were actually better learners of traditional academic skills than children without preschool experience. Perhaps the slight aptitude and achievement edge which the experimental group maintained over the control group through the early elementary years had a cumulative effect upon measured achievement.

Did preschool have different impacts on different kinds of children?

The Perry Project sample was relatively more homogeneous than the samples selected for most preschool research as a result of narrow restrictions placed upon entering Binet IQ and family SES. Consequently, interactions of treatment with child characteristics were rather unlikely to appear.

One important finding, however, did emerge. Children in the experimental group from the lowest SES homes and ostensibly "least supportive" environments may have gained somewhat more from the preschool experience than their slightly more advantaged peers. This trend appeared in both academic achievement and actual school success as indicated by multiple linear regression analyses of the interactions between treatment group membership and home environment factors. In sum, preschool seems to have put children from different home environments on a somewhat more equal footing with respect to their ability to cope with the demands of elementary school.

Is preschool a good investment?

Acknowledging the findings of this and other studies that preschool can benefit individual children, there remains the question whether improved test performance or even greater success in school is adequate justification for vast expenditures of resources in early childhood education. The importance of school achievement for life success has been severely questioned in recent years (e.g., McClelland, 1973, and Jencks et al., 1972). Moreover, strong arguments have been made that disproportionately large numbers of minority-group children are classified as "educable mentally retarded" and placed in special education programs when in fact they function quite adequately in their own social-cultural spheres (Mercer, 1971). In the continuing longitudinal study of children in the Perry

Project sample, information about children's social adjustment and accomplishments outside of school (among peers, in the family, and in the
larger community) is being collected. These data will provide a basis for
assessing outcomes which have broad individual and sociological
implications.

Even at this juncture, however, some conclusions can be reached
about the economic returns upon the investment made in the Perry Preschool. A recent study by Weber, Foster, and Weikart (1978) analyzed
the economic impact of the Perry Project. This analysis found that *there
was more than complete recovery of the total cost of the preschool project*
from savings which accrued because experimental-group children required less costly forms of education during their school years and because of better educational progress by experimental-group children
which predicts slightly higher lifetime earnings.

> For the subjects with two years of preschool compensatory education, the
> social rate of return (economic benefit) to investment in the Ypsilanti Perry
> Preschool Project was 3.7% (one year returned 9.7%) . . . There is justifica-
> tion for public investment projects such as the Ypsilanti Perry Preschool
> Project . . . which lead to more than complete recovery of the costs.

What makes a preschool program effective?

The Perry Preschool was successful: it not only benefited individual
children over the long-run but apparently did so at a cost savings to
society. Why did this project succeed when so many others have not?
Although we cannot answer this question with certainty, it seems important to examine our hunches.

Characteristics of children served

It may well be that preschool programs are most effective for children who
are the most economically disadvantaged and farthest removed from the
cultural mainstream by virtue of language and/or ethnicity. This is not a
finding of the Perry Project, but it is a hypothesis that generally fits our
organizational experience over the past fifteen years implementing educational programs for children throughout this country and in Latin
America.

Special challenge of educational innovation

The Perry Project was a unique undertaking with a special sense of
mission; project staff were by all accounts in the "avant-garde" of early
childhood education. There was, undoubtedly, a "Hawthorne" effect
operating in the early days of the project. However, the project continued
over a five-year period, and any "Hawthorne" effect must at least have
been muted by time as the staff's initial exhilaration gave way to mature

professionalism. Similarly for children, the novelty and specialness of preschool must have waned over the course of two years in the project. In sum, the success of the Perry Preschool Project may have been in part, though not large part, the product of novelty and excitement associated with the experiment itself.

Delivery system variables

Probably of greatest importance to the success of this and other preschool projects were variables in the system by which the educational program was delivered. Several major factors in the delivery system are discussed briefly below.

Relationship to school system. The Perry Preschool Project was part of the special services division within the schools, an office organized directly under the superintendent and comprising special educators, social workers, and psychologists. Since the division was relatively new, most staff were new to the school system. Operating directly under the superintendent, the project was relatively independent of building principals and the schools' business office. In addition to these organizational-administrative advantages, the project operated in a setting relatively free of the political machinations so common in large urban school systems. These factors contributed much to the stability of the project over its five years of operation.

Research and development component. There was a fundamental commitment to research and development. Project staff wore more than one "hat". Teachers not only taught, but helped to develop curriculum. Research and supervisory staff likewise participated in the development effort. Outside consultants were brought in to review progress, advise, and debate. Self-evaluation and problem-solving by teachers were intensive throughout the project and, together with a sense of accountability created by ongoing evaluation of the program, certainly contributed to its success.

Public accountability. The project also responded to the outside world of curious professionals, students, and members of the community. Although it was often difficult to meet the expectations of the large numbers of people who wanted to visit the project, such pressures kept staff "on display" and in daily contact with the wider world of education. The presence of inquisitive visitors—international scholars, high-ranking officials, educators, concerned parents—creates a setting in which teaching cannot be mechanical, in which every action requires explanation. Conference presentations to skeptical professional audiences provided additional contact with the field and created additional pressures for accountability. These contacts with the outside world, even more than formal evaluation activities, keep the importance of what one is trying to do in focus and encourage self-appraisal and development. The preschool teacher or supervisor is unlikely to maintain high quality performance without such support.

Formal curriculum model. Although it evolved substantially over the course of five years, a formal curriculum model guided teaching activity throughout the project. A formal curriculum is a conceptual framework with articulated decision-rules which not only shapes educational practice but permits systematic, objective evaluation of teaching activity. While such a model is obviously essential to dissemination of a preschool program, it also appears to be vital to the success of an ongoing program. Without a well articulated curriculum framework, self-evaluation by teachers and supervision of teachers tends to be unsystematic, and educational practice in the classroom, inconsistent.

Home teaching component. Although the home teaching component of the preschool program was not experimentally evaluated by working with some parents of preschoolers and not others, project staff felt strongly that contact with parents and children in the context of the home was important for *teachers*. The knowledge that teachers gained of children as members of families and neighborhoods—as individuals with special interests, unique experiences, and idiosyncratic behaviors—helped guide educational decision-making in the classroom, contributing importantly to the individualization of the educational program. Moreover, it seems likely that opportunities to know teachers within the context of their own homes gave *parents* a new perspective on education and perhaps helped to reduce the discontinuities between school and home traditionally characteristic of the population served. In short, though we have no hard, quantitative evidence that home teaching was crucial to the success of the project, both project staff and parents would argue for its importance.

Teacher evaluation and planning time. Perhaps most frequently overlooked by educational programs and school systems is the significance of teacher evaluation and planning time. Unlike many projects, the Perry Preschool provided large blocks of time for team evaluation and planning by teachers. Each teacher taught in the classroom for five half-days and made about five 90-minute home visits each week. The remainder of each teacher's work week was spent in evaluation and planning activities, alone and with other project staff. In the typical preschool intervention, children's in-school time is maximized in the hope of maximizing program impact; however, quantity and quality of education are not always highly, or even positively, correlated in the real world. Projects which maximize direct child services may often deliver the least effective programs. To remain productive and effective, teachers apparently need large amounts of time away from children for reflection and problem-solving.

What next?

Although no definitive answers are proposed regarding the ingredients of successful preschool programs, some characteristics have been suggested. The results of the Perry Preschool Project strongly suggest that *under certain conditions* preschool education can be so effective that it would be negligent for government and the private sector not to provide preschool services to economically disadvantaged children. At issue, of course, is the definition of those "certain conditions".

Are some curricula more effective than others?

It is important to determine whether different educational approaches—curricula and their resulting educational processes—have different patterns and magnitudes of impact upon children. A number of recent studies at both the preschool and elementary levels have examined the questions of differential curriculum impat (Weikart et al., 1978; Karnes, 1973; Smith, 1973; Weisberg, 1974; Miller and Dyer, 1975; Stallings, 1975; Bennett et al., 1976). In general, the findings for preschool indicate that the closer the project is to a true experiment in sample assignment and, particularly, *curriculum control*, the more similar are the impacts of different curricula.

A major impediment to research on differential curricular impacts is the lack of instrumentation permitting fine-grained analyses of child outcomes along diverse dimensions. Adequate measures of problem-solving ability, communicative competence, creativity, self-concept, responsibility, and so forth are largely primitive or nonexistent. Thus, educational evaluation continues to rely primarily upon traditional tests of aptitude and achievement, all of which measure very nearly the same thing. Although current interest in the development of more adequate measures is high, relatively little progress has been made to date. At present, little is known with confidence about the effects of systematically different preschool experiences. Finding the answers represents a major challenge for those who wish to implement effective educational programs.

How do delivery system variables influence program effectiveness?

The systems by which educational programs are delivered have received relatively little attention in efforts to evaluate preschool education. Traditionally the child has been the focus of our attention; educational process and delivery system variables have typically received only cursory mention in our descriptions of research design. It has become increasingly obvious in recent years to those involved in providing educational services that the organization of educational systems, the management of projects, staff training systems, evaluation procedures, differential access to decision-making, problem-raising/solving procedures, and a multitude of other delivery system variables bear importantly upon the educational experiences of children and the ultimate impact of educational programs.

As suggested in the preceding section, the success of the Perry Preschool Project may well have been a function of such delivery system characteristics as: a high degree of organizational autonomy; continuous and adequate financing; the integration of research and development with teaching; the presence of a formal curriculum model to guide training, classroom decision-making, and quality control; the explicit provision of evaluation/planning time for teachers; openness and accountability to the public; and home teaching which involved parents more directly in the educational process. Far better understanding than we have now of educational delivery systems is required if we are to fashion new educational systems which are viable in real-world settings and maximize benefits to children.

Conclusion

The Ypsilanti Perry Preschool Project was designed to help economically disadvantaged children at high academic risk cope more effectively with school and adult life in the mainstream of this society. The original project and longitudinal follow-up have consumed fifteen years to this point. In four more years the full sample will be out of high school with one year of experience in the "real world" or college, as the case may be. The interim data reported here are striking. Experimental-group children have been significantly more successful in coping with the demands of school as judged by their performance on achievement tests, teachers' ratings of their social-emotional adjustment, and, most importantly, their actual success in school defined in terms of grade and class placement. Moreover, a social-benefit cost analysis indicates that differences in achievement and grade placement favoring the experimental group are sufficient to guarantee more than complete recovery of the initial costs of preschool. Whether the impact of preschool, mediated of course by many intervening variables, will persist or even increase in certain areas remains to be seen as the longitudinal study continues.

We have in the past expected too much of early childhood education. With the advent of the Great Society's War on Poverty, we hoped to undo the effects of economic disadvantage and assimilate ethnic minorities into the mainstream by providing compensatory preschool programs for the children of poverty. This hope did not materialize, and the backlash generated by the revelations of the Westinghouse-Ohio University report (Cicirelli, 1969) almost destroyed Head Start as a national program. Fortunately Head Start and publicly supported preschool programs in general were saved by parents and educators who recognized the potential of early childhood education. Now our task is to design educational systems which can realize that potential for all children, recognizing, however, that educational programs, no matter how effective, do not eliminate the need for broader social-economic change.

Appendix A: Measurement

Measures of aptitude and achievement: preschool period

Four standardized tests were employed during the preschool period to assess a broad spectrum of cognitive and linguistic skills:

- Stanford-Binet Intelligence Scale (Binet)
- Arthur Adaptation of the Leiter International Performance Scale (Leiter)
- Peabody Picture Vocabulary Test (PPVT)
- Illinois Test of Psycholinguistic Abilities, Experimental Edition (ITPA)

Scores on these tests were assumed to predict how well children were likely to do in school rather than measure psychological traits such as "intelligence" (see discussion in chapter I).

Binet

The Binet (Terman and Merrill, 1960) was considered the primary index of academic potential because of its demonstrated relationship with school achievement and its widespread use in other educational research. Of the four standardized tests employed, only the Binet was administered prior to project enrollment (pre-FEY, Table 7) and consistently thereafter through fourth grade. Since the Binet is a common denominator of so many studies assessing the concurrent validity of other measures, it will serve as the criterion in estimating the concurrent validity of Leiter, PPVT, and ITPA scores for the project sample.

Leiter

The Leiter is a completely nonverbal, individual test which presents the child with a sequence of increasingly complex classification-seriation problems. According to its author the Arthur Adaptation "is, in principle, a nonverbal Binet Scale for young children" (Arthur, 1952, p. 3). Although there is some evidence in the literature (Bensberg and Sloan, 1951; Beverly and Bensberg, 1950; Orgel and Dreger, 1955; Tate, 1952) that Leiter and Binet performances are moderately to strongly correlated, the tests are clearly not interchangeable. There seems to have been little previous use of the Leiter in educational research with preschool-age children. The Leiter was administered to all children (EXP and CON) within three months after project enrollment (post-FEY, Table 7) and every spring thereafter through third grade (with the exception of Waves 0 and 1 at SEY). Scores were obtained by dividing mental age (from Arthur, 1952) by chronological age.

PPVT

The PPVT is an individual test of receptive vocabulary and visual decoding in which the examiner reads a sequence of stimulus words and the subject chooses one of four pictures which best illustrates each word (Dunn, 1965). Form A of the PPVT was administered to all children within three months after entry (post-FEY, Table 7) and every spring thereafter through third grade (with the exception of Waves 0 and 1 at SEY). PPVT scores were obtained by dividing mental age (from Dunn, 1965) by chronological age, producing a more continuous distribution of scores than would have resulted using the "deviation IQs" provided in the test manual.[1]

ITPA

The ITPA (Experimental Version, McCarthy and Kirk, 1961) comprises nine subtests, each intended to tap a particular dimension of general cognitive/linguistic ability. Table A-1 provides brief descriptions of each subtest. The degree to which they assess discrete cognitive and communi-

Table A-1
Descriptions of ITPA Subtests

- *Auditory-Vocal Automatic (AVAU):* ability to complete a statement by supplying the grammatically correct word
- *Visual Decoding (VD):* ability to select one picture from a set of four which is most structurally similar to a stimulus picture
- *Motor Encoding (ME):* ability to look at a picture of an object and to pantomine the appropriate motion for its manipulation
- *Auditory-Vocal Association (AVAS):* ability to complete verbal analogies
- *Visual-Motor Sequential (VMS):* ability to reproduce sequences of visual stimuli (small chips containing a picture or geometric form) after five seconds exposure to a model
- *Vocal-Encoding (VE):* ability to verbally describe simple objects
- *Visual-Motor Association (VMA):* ability to select one picture from a set of four which is most functionally or conceptually similar to a stimulus picture
- *Auditory Decoding (AD):* ability to understand the meanings of spoken words, requiring a simple yes or no answer to a question of the form "Do (Noun) (Verb)?"
- *Auditory Vocal Sequential (AVS):* ability to verbally repeat a number series (short-term memory)

[1]Deviation scores from the test manual are computed for six-month intervals through age five and for one-year intervals thereafter. Within these broad age bands, the same raw scores produce the same deviation scores regardless of age. Since the age range of project children at each testpoint was restricted to a 12-month interval and the distribution of their raw scores was relatively narrow, ratio scores more finely differentiated their performance than deviation scores would have. Although the ratio scores reported here are not perfectly comparable to deviation scores reported elsewhere, correlations of about .90 between ratio and deviation scores have been obtained in analyses of data from another preschool project conducted by the High/Scope Foundation.

cative skills, as opposed to general ability, is uncertain and may, in fact, vary from one population to another (Leventhal and Stedman, 1967). The ITPA was administered to all children within three months after project enrollment (post-FEY, Table 7). Although not given at SEY, it was administered annually through third grade to children in all waves. Raw scores on each subtest and the total battery were converted to Language Age scores using tables in the ITPA manual (McCarthy and Kirk, 1961).

Reliability and validity of standardized tests

It is difficult to make meaningful comparisons between reliability/validity estimates derived from project data and the results of other studies, since sample characteristics, scoring procedures, and reliability and validity coefficients vary widely. However, the most widely used tests of those considered here (Binet, PPVT, and ITPA) are reported to have relatively high reliability and concurrent validity.[2] Although limited information on the Leiter suggests that its reliability and concurrent validity (with Binet as the criterion) are comparable, it has not been subjected to the same scrutiny as the other instruments.[3] Test-retest correlations and estimates of concurrent validity (Binet as criterion) derived from data collected on the Perry sample are reported here in order that the interested reader may pursue these questions further. Complete intercorrelation matrices for all instruments at and across all testpoints are provided in the *Statistical Supplement*, Part B.

Test-retest correlation coefficients for the preschool period were computed separately for the experimental (N=58) and control (N=65) groups since performance stability might have been affected by treatment. Pearson product-moment correlation coefficients for the FEY-SEY and SEY-S2Y (FEY-S2Y for the ITPA) data collection intervals are reported by treatment group in Table A-2A. With the exception of FEY-SEY PPVT in the experimental group, all correlations reached statistical significance at the .05 level. Binet and Leiter correlations were somewhat higher in the experimental group; PPVT and ITPA correlations, in the control group. The only statistically significant difference between the two treatment groups occurred in PPVT scores over the FEY-SEY interval. It should be noted that coefficients obtained for the Perry sample are somewhat lower than many reported in the literature due probably to the restricted age and performance range of children in this sample and to the long test-retest interval.

---

[2]Recent reviews of Binet and PPVT reliability and validity (focusing on preschool-age children) appear in *The Quality of the Head Start Planned Variation Data* (Walker, Bane and Bryk, 1973). For a more general, albeit less up-to-date, summary of PPVT reliability and validity the reader is referred to the test manual (Dunn, 1965). The best single source for information on the ITPA is a report by the test developers (McCarthy and Kirk, 1963).

[3]Reliability and validity data for the Leiter (both Leiter's 1948 revision and Arthur's 1952 adaptation) are sparse, particularly in the case of preschool-age children. The best single source for references to studies utilizing the Leiter scales and for summary reliability/validity data is a recent doctoral dissertation by Gretzler (1973).

Concurrent validity was estimated by correlating Leiter, PPVT, and ITPA scores with Binet scores at each testpoint during the preschool period. Correlation coefficients are presented separately for the two treatment groups in Table A-2B. With the exception of FEY ITPA in the control group, all coefficients reached significance at the .05 level. Although the Leiter, PPVT, and ITPA were not redundant with the Binet, concurrent correlations increased substantially from FEY to S2Y. As with reliability estimates, concurrent validity estimates for the project sample are often lower than would be obtained in a sample not so restricted in age and performance range.

Table A-2

Instrument Reliability and Validity for the Perry Sample

A. Test-Retest Reliability Estimates for Indices of Academic Potential

INSTRUMENT	GROUP	Test-Retest Interval	
		FEY — (8 mos) — SEY	(12 mos) — S2Y
BINET	EXP	.56*	.65*
	CON	.41*	.53*
LEITER	EXP	.46*	.50*
	CON	.44*	.56*
PPVT	EXP	.22	.47*
	CON	.61*	.70*
ITPA-TOTAL	EXP	.47* †	
	CON	.68* †	

†The ITPA was not administered at SEY, therefore reliability can only be estimated over the 20-month interval from FEY to SEY.

*Asterisks indicate significance level (*p<.10; **p<.05; ***p<.01). If no asterisks appear, the difference is not significant at or beyond the .10 level.*

B. Concurrent Validity of Indices of Academic Potential: Binet as Criterion

INSTRUMENT	GROUP	Concurrent Binet		
		FEY	SEY	S2Y
LEITER	EXP	.29*	.55*	.50*
	CON	.25*	.40*	.37*
PPVT	EXP	.45*	.38*	.57*
	CON	.38*	.48*	.54*
ITPA-TOTAL	EXP	.28*	——	.42*
	CON	−.08	——	.51*

*Asterisks indicate significance level (*p<.10; **p<.05; ***p<.01). If no asterisks appear, the difference is not significant at or beyond the .10 level.*

Measures of aptitude and achievement: post-treatment period

The four standardized tests used during the preschool period (Binet, Leiter, PPVT, and ITPA) were also administered to experimental and control children during the post-treatment (elementary school) period. In addition, three other instruments were used to measure academic aptitude and achievement:

- California Achievement Test, Lower and Upper Primary Forms (CAT)
- Pupil Behavior Inventory, Academic Motivation Scale (PBI-AM)
- Ypsilanti Rating Scale—Academic Potential and Verbal Skill Scales (YRS-AP and YRS-VS)

Since the Binet, Leiter, PPVT, and ITPA have already been described, they will only be given brief consideration here. The CAT, PBI-AM, YRS-AP, and YRS-VS will be examined more thoroughly.

Binet, Leiter, PPVT, and ITPA

All four instruments were administered and scored as they had been during the preschool period. The Leiter, PPVT, and ITPA were administered at SKG through S3G; the Binet, at SKG through S4G. Test-retest correlation coefficients for the elementary school period (Table A-3) were generally higher than those obtained for the preschool years. The patterns of one-year test-retest correlations were quite similar for the experimental and control groups. With some exceptions correlation coefficients were strong (>.50), falling in the .60s through .80s for the Binet and .50s through .70s for the Leiter, PPVT, and ITPA. Although test-retest reliabilities are not as high as some reported in the literature, they seem quite adequate particularly in light of the restricted age and performance ranges of children in this sample and the length of test-retest intervals. Concurrent validity was estimated by correlating measures of academic potential with Binet and California Achievement Test (CAT) scores and by factor analysis. The results of these analyses will be considered following a discussion of the remaining measures of academic potential.

California Achievement Tests (CAT)

The first two levels of the CAT were employed: the Lower Primary at S1G and S2G and the Upper Primary at S3G and S4G. Both levels contain three subject-area tests: Reading, Arithmetic, and Language. Each subject-area test in turn comprises two subtests; these are described briefly in Table A-4. The CAT tests were administered by trained testers, generally persons with teacher certification, to small groups (5-10) of children. Normally two of the subject-area tests were administered at one testing session and the third at a different session. Scores for each subject-area test were computed by adding raw scores from the two subtests. The CAT total score was obtained by summing all six subtest scores.

Table A-3

Test-Retest Correlations of Elementary School Measures for the Perry Sample

Indices of Academic Potential

	ONE-YEAR TEST-RETEST INTERVALS									
	EXPERIMENTAL GROUP					CONTROL GROUP				
INSTRUMENT	(S2Y)—SKG	SKG—S1G	S1G—S2G	S2G—S3G	S3G—S4G	(S2Y)—SKG	SKG—S1G	S1G—S2G	S2G—S3G	S3G—S4G
BINET	.70*	.80*	.69*	.81*	.74*	.61*	.77*	.66*	.71*	.75*
LEITER	.43*	.60*	.50*	.58*	—	.37*	.65*	.73*	.68*	—
PPVT	.59*	.66*	.65*	.67*	—	.70*	.51*	.58*	.59*	—
ITPA-TOTAL	.53*	.68*	.68*	.70*	—	.61*	.66*	.55*	.56*	—
ITPA-AVAS	.53*	.57*	.49*	.70*	—	.60*	.51*	.53*	.46*	—
CAT-TOTAL	—	—	.76*	.82*	.81*	—	—	.67*	.80*	.87*
CAT-Reading	—	—	.80*	.85*	.77*	—	—	.69*	.74*	.74*
CAT-Arithmetic	—	—	.65*	.75*	.72*	—	—	.63*	.68*	.86*
CAT-Language	—	—	.64*	.65*	.82*	—	—	.31*	.69*	.75*
PBI-AM	—	.41*	.52*	.62*	—	—	.61*	.61*	.33	—
YRS-AP	—	.53*	.64*	.39*	—	—	.67*	.62*	.63*	—
YRS-VS	—	.25	.38*	.48*	—	—	.63*	.53*	.49*	—

Asterisks indicate significance level (*p<.10; **p<.05; ***p<.01). If no asterisks appear, the difference is not significant at or beyond the .10 level.

Table A-4

*Descriptions of CAT Subtests for the Lower Primary (LP)
and the Upper Primary (UP) Levels*

CAT READING TEST
_____

- *Reading Vocabulary*

  LP: Four sections require ability to: 1) determine if two words written in different type face are the same or different; 2) choose the one word pronounced by the examiner from three words written in the answer booklet; 3) match a written keyword with the one of three written words which is opposite in meaning; and 4) select written words or phrases which best describe a picture.

  UP: Two sections similar to sections 2 and 3 of the LP Level contain more difficult items.

- *Reading Comprehension*

  LP: One section requires ability to follow specific directions and interpret written material.

  UP: Three sections require ability to: 1) follow directions; 2) interpret dictionary information, use indices, tables of contents, and graphs, and alphabetize; and 3) read brief stories and identify topics or central ideas, sequences of events, etc.

CAT ARITHMETIC TEST
_____

- *Arithmetic Reasoning*

  LP: Two sections require: 1) knowledge of basic arithmetic concepts and 2) solutions to simple problems read by the examiner.

  UP: Two sections are similar to those of the LP Level but contain more difficult items. A third section requires comprehension of signs and symbols used to express arithmetic processes, measures of time, money, weight, and distance.

- *Arithmetic Fundamentals*

  LP: Two sections include: 1) 25 addition problems and 2) 20 subtraction problems.

  UP: Four sections include: 50 problems each for addition, subtraction, multiplication, and division.

CAT LANGUAGE TEST
_____

- *Mechanics of English*

  LP: Three sections require knowledge of: 1) capitalization; 2) punctuation (periods, commas, question marks); and 3) proper word usage (tense, person, number, and case).

  UP: The same three sections contain more advanced items.

- *Spelling*

  LP: The examiner pronounces 20 words for the child to write.
  UP: The examiner pronounces 25 words for the child to write.

Limited reliability and validity information presented in the test manuals (Tiegs and Clark, 1957a and 1957b) suggests that all CAT tests have high internal reliability and adequate construct validity as judged by the correlation of CAT subtest scores with children's performance on other achievement tests. Test-retest correlations are reported in Table A-3 for both the experimental and the control group. The intercorrelations of CAT tests over one-year intervals are comparable for the two treatment groups and strong (.60s through .80s) with the exception of Language Test scores for the control group from S1G-S2G ($r = .31$). Correlations for the S2G-S3G interval are as high as those for other intervals, indicating that Lower and Upper Primary levels of the CAT ranked children similarly.

Intercorrelations of CAT subject-area tests and correlations of each test with the total score are reported in the *Statistical Supplement* (Part B, Tables 3 and 4) for experimental and control groups at all testpoints. Not surprisingly, Reading and Language tests were more highly correlated with one another than with the Arithmetic test. All tests were strongly correlated (.81-.97) with the CAT total score.

Pupil Behavior Inventory (PBI)

The PBI is described by its authors (Vinter, Sarri, Vorwaller, and Schafer, 1966) as a standardized rating scale developed for:

> ... measuring the extent of Pupil conformity to the behavior standards maintained both officially and unofficially by school personnel. It provides a measure of those behavioral and attitudinal factors which affect the degree of success a pupil will have in accomplishing his educational objectives. (p. 1)

The instrument comprises 34 items describing various behaviors which may be assessed by teachers in normal classroom settings. Factor analyses of these items by the authors produced five PBI factors. Only one factor, Academic Motivation and Performance (PBI-AM), deals specifically with academic behavior; it is considered a measure of academic potential in this study. Actual items making up the PBI-AM factor are presented in Table A-5. The remaining four PBI factors are measures of social-emotional development and will be examined later in this section.

Table A-5

*Items from PBI and YRS Factors
Used as Indices of Academic Potential*

*PUPIL BEHAVIOR INVENTORY:
Academic Motivation Factor (AM)*

- Shows initiative
- Alert and interested in school work
- Learning retained well
- Completes assignments
- Motivated toward academic performance
- Positive concern for own education
- Hesitant to try, or gives up easily
- Uninterested in subject matter
- Shows positive leadership

YPSILANTI RATING SCALE: Academic Potential FACTOR (AP)

- Degree of imagination and creativity shown in handling
    materials and equipment
- Level of academic readiness
- Prediction of future academic success

YPSILANTI RATING SCALE: Verbal Skill Factor (VS)

- Level of verbal communication

PBI data were collected from teachers of Perry sample children at four points: SKG, S1G, S2G, and S3G. Teachers received one form for each child in the sample and were asked to rate each child on every item according to whether the behavior described occurred "very frequently", "frequently", "sometimes", "infrequently", or "very infrequently". Items from the five factors were interspersed with one another. About one-quarter of the items were positively worded; the remainder, negatively worded. Each item received a 1 to 5 score, 5 denoting the "positive" end of the scale. Factor scores were computed by obtaining the mean score of all items associated with each factor.

PBI-AM one-year test-retest correlation coefficients for the Perry sample ranged from .41 through .62 in the experimental group and from .33 through .61 in the control group (Table A-3).[4] These correlations are surprisingly strong considering that rating categories were not described in great detail and that teachers had to determine for themselves what specific frequency of occurrence merited a "frequently" as opposed to "sometimes". Correlations between the PBI-AM factor and other PBI factors are reported in the *Statistical Supplement* (Part B, Tables 7 and 8); they tend to be moderate to high.

Ypsilanti Rating Scale (YRS)

The Ypsilanti Rating Scale (YRS) was developed by project staff during the first few years of the project. Two versions of the instrument were constructed: the first for preschool teachers to rate experimental group children and their mothers during their participation in the project; the second for elementary school teachers to rate both experimental and control group children during the early elementary grades. Since this report focuses on comparisons of the two treatment groups, the preschool version, for which data were limited to the experimental group, is not considered here.

YRS instructions ask teachers to rate children on eleven subscales describing academic and social adjustment within the classroom setting. An additional two subscales required teachers to evaluate maternal involvement with the schools. Although teachers only rated children in their classes who belonged to the Perry sample, they were asked to compare each child to be rated with every other child in their classrooms. A seven-point rating scale was used with high scores representing positive evaluations. The five YRS factors were derived from a principal component analysis followed by a Varimax rotation of factors with eigenvalues greater than 1.0. Only data collected in 1967 on Waves 0 through 4 (EXP and CON; N=65) were used in this analysis. Factor scores were computed by averaging the scores of the subscales associated with each factor.

Of the five YRS factors, two are explicit measures of academic potential: YRS Academic Potential Factor (YRS-AP) and YRS Verbal Skills Factor (YRS-VS). Two remaining factors are ostensibly measures of social

---

[4]Additional reliability and validity data are reported by the authors (Vinter et al., 1966).

adjustment and will be described more fully with other measures of socio-emotional development. The fifth factor is an unsuccessful measure of mothers' actual and predicted involvement with the schools; it will not be given further consideration in this report.

The items making up the YRS-AP and YRS-VS factors are presented in Table A-5. The intercorrelations of ratings made by different teachers over one-year intervals are reported in Table A-3. With the exception of the YRS-VS factor from SKG to S1G in the experimental group, coefficients are surprisingly large (comparable to those obtained for standardized measures) and generally significant (p<.05), indicating both the reliability of the instrument and the relative stability of children's behavior over time.

Interrelationship of aptitude and achievement measures

Binet and CAT-Total scores were selected as criterion measures for estimating the concurrent validity of aptitude and achievement measures for the Perry sample. Correlations are reported in Table A-6. The criterion measures themselves tended to correlate strongly: .51 through .63 in the experimental group and .44 through .57 in the control group. Only the Leiter and the YRS-VS did not evidence consistently strong concurrent correlations with either of the criterion measures. The PPVT, ITPA-Total, and ITPA-AVAS correlated most highly with the Binet. CAT subtests, PBI-AM, and YRS-AP correlated most strongly with the CAT-Total, though their correlations with concurrent Binet scores were also moderate to high in both the experimental and control groups.

Table A-6

Concurrent Validity of Indices of Academic Potential for the Perry Sample: Elementary School Period

A. Correlation with Concurrent Binet Scores

INSTRUMENT	EXPERIMENTAL GROUP					CONTROL GROUP				
	SKG	S1G	S2G	S3G	S4G	SKG	S1G	S2G	S3G	S4G
LEITER	.41*	.49*	.51*	.35*	——	.49*	.40*	.52*	.63*	——
PPVT	.70*	.60*	.53*	.50*	——	.58*	.71*	.48*	.50*	——
ITPA-TOTAL	.63*	.69*	.68*	.69*	——	.52*	.55*	.57*	.58*	——
ITPA-AVAS	.57*	.61*	.62*	.55*	——	.54*	.60*	.43*	.62*	——
CAT-TOTAL	——	.59*	.51*	.63*	.63*	——	.57*	.44*	.53*	.51*
CAT-Reading	——	.51*	.48*	.60*	.61*	——	.48*	.36*	.34*	.53*
CAT-Arithmetic	——	.51*	.55*	.60*	.59*	——	.55*	.47*	.56*	.47*
CAT-Language	——	.56*	.34*	.50*	.58*	——	.45*	.32*	.46*	.45*
PBI-AM	.42*	.35*	.38*	.39*	——	.57*	.43*	.50*	.26	——
YRS-AP	.39*	.27	.34*	.46*	——	.53*	.49*	.48*	.45*	——
YRS-VS	.42*	.10	.31*	.50*	——	.45*	.55*	.29*	.11	——

B. Correlation with Concurrent CAT Total Scores

INSTRUMENT	EXPERIMENTAL GROUP				CONTROL GROUP			
	S1G	S2G	S3G	S4G	S1G	S2G	S3G	S4G
BINET	.59*	.51*	.63*	.63*	.57*	.44*	.53*	.51*
LEITER	.36*	.49*	.37*	——	.54*	.45*	.56*	——
PPVT	.30*	.29*	.27*	——	.35*	.13	.07	——
ITPA-TOTAL	.51*	.35*	.42*	——	.43*	.29*	.26	——
ITPA-AVAS	.49*	.56*	.52*	——	.42*	.26	.30*	——
CAT-Reading	.90*	.95*	.91*	.93*	.89*	.91*	.91*	.93*
CAT-Arithmetic	.88*	.89*	.93*	.96*	.87*	.91*	.97*	.97*
CAT-Language	.86*	.89*	.86*	.92*	.81*	.88*	.91*	.91*
PBI-AM	.49*	.71*	.63*	——	.62*	.74*	.54*	——
YRS-AP	.50*	.68*	.50*	——	.60*	.57*	.67*	——
YRS-VS	.31*	.38*	.44*	——	.51*	.33*	.17	——

The relationships among measures of aptitude and achievement were further examined using factor analysis.[5] Table A-7A presents the results of three-factor principal component analyses of all measures (excluding ITPA and CAT subtests) for the total sample at SKG through S3G.[6] The first principal component at each testpoint accounts for about 50% of the variance in measures of academic potential. This, in conjunction with consistently high loadings (>.50) by all variables on the first component, indicates a strong general factor among measures of aptitude and achievement. Stated differently, to an important degree the Binet, Leiter, PPVT, ITPA, CAT, PBI-AM, YRS-AP, and YRS-VS measure the same thing.

At the same time, however, these measures are not equivalent. Three-factor Varimax rotations of the principal component structures at SKG through S3G are presented in Table A-7B. Binet, PPVT, and ITPA consistently load together on the same factor, while the Leiter loads on a separate factor and the PBI-AM, YRS-AP, and YRS-VS on yet another factor. The CAT-Total is not unambiguously associated with any factor across time, loading with the Leiter at S1G and S3G and with PBI-A, YRS-AP, and YRS-VS at S2G. These three factors together account for about 80% of the variance in measures of academic potential at each testpoint.

Table A-7C presents the results of a Varimax rotation of only the first two principal components. Binet, PPVT, and ITPA again load together on the same factor; the PBI-AM, YRS-AP, and YRS-VS, on the other. The Leiter loads about equally on both factors with the exception of S1G when it is most closely associated with Binet, PPVT, and ITPA. The CAT, however, tends to be associated most strongly with the teacher ratings except at S1G when it loads equally on the two factors.

Thus, the Binet, PPVT, and ITPA seem to hang together as measures of general cognitive-linguistic skills and the CAT and teacher ratings as measures of more specific academic skills, while the Leiter remains something of an enigma. In short, while it seems legitimate to group these eight measures for purposes of reporting general findings of the study, it should not be assumed that they measure equally the same dimensions of children's behavior.

Measures of home environment

Three home environment measures appear in analyses of data from the preschool period:

- Perry Demographic Questionnaire (PDQ)

---

[5]At no testpoint could more than three principal components with eigenvalues greater than 1.0 be extracted, and at three of four testpoints the third factors had eigenvalues somewhat less than 1.0. Although the third principal component does not meet stringent reliability criteria in all analyses, its consideration for exploratory purposes seems warranted.

[6]S4G data were not analyzed since only the Binet and CAT were administered at this testpoint.

- Cognitive Home Environment Scale (CHES)
- Maternal Attitude Inventory (MAI)

They are considered in relationship to the experimental design in chapter I.

PDQ

The PDQ interview schedule was developed by project staff for the collection of basic demographic data on all project families prior to enrollment. Descriptive statistics derived from PDQ data are reported in the "Sample" section of chapter I (Tables 3, 5, and 6). Two PDC variables were included as predictors in the regression analyses presented in chapter II: Socio-Economic Status[7] (SES) and Mother's Education (MO. EDUC.).

CHES

The Cognitive Home Environment Scale (CHES) originally consisted of 25 interview questions[8] derived from the more than 60 questions on R. M. Wolf's Environmental Process Scale (1964). The CHES was intended to measure factors in home environments which directly influenced child development. On the basis of previous research (Dave, 1963; Wolf, 1964), it was anticipated that this measure of environment would be more strongly related to developmental and school achievement measures than would more global environmental indices like SES, particularly within the "homogeneously" low SES project sample.

Among measures considered in this study the CHES is an anomaly. It was developed late in the project and was administered to all mothers in a single calender year (1966) rather than at a single testpoint.[9] Consequently, children from different waves were of different ages when data were collected. Wave 0 was in second grade; Wave 1, in first grade; Wave 2, in kindergarten; and Waves 3 and 4, not yet in school. Although the CHES was neither a true preschool-period nor post-treatment measure, it will be considered along with preschool-period measures in order to address issues raised by its inclusion in regression analyses predicting preschool Binet performance.

The CHES factors analyzed in this volume are rather different from those in the 1970 Perry Report. Re-examination of the raw data uncovered problems of coding reliability and revealed that on certain items maternal response patterns were related to age of child. Consequently, age-sensitive items were eliminated and other items recoded when necessary. Next, CHES data were factor analyzed to determine whether a meaningful simple structure underlay the remaining items. Ultimately, ten of the original 25 items were retained; these are briefly described in Table A-8. A Varimax rotation of the first two factors from a principal components analysis of these ten items produced the most parsimonious and interpret-

---

[7]The SES index used in this study is fully described in the "Sample" section of chapter I.

[8]The original CHES is reproduced in the 1970 Perry Report, appendix D (Weikart, Deloria, Lawser, and Wiegerink, 1970).

[9]In the experimental design of this study, a single testpoint spans a period of five years as each of five waves moves through a given grade level (cf. Tables 1 and 2, chapter I).

Table A-7

Results of Factor Analysis of Indices of Academic Potential: SKG-S3G

A. *Principal Components*

VARIABLE	SKG (N=114)			S1G (N=93)			S2G (N=76)			S3G (N=72)		
	F1	F2	F3	F1	F2	F3	F1	F2	F3	F1	F2	F3
ITPA-TOTAL	.73	.36	-.11	.72	-.41	.12	.62	-.62	-.02	.63	.54	.07
PPVT	.68	.51	.31	.64	-.52	.39	.56	-.56	.39	.52	.52	.49
BINET	.80	.38	.06	.80	-.42	.07	.75	-.44	-.16	.75	.47	-.12
LEITER	.64	.01	-.68	.65	-.20	-.59	.60	-.03	-.68	.64	.05	-.52
CAT-TOTAL	—	—	—	.78	.01	-.36	.79	.27	-.17	.74	-.09	-.43
YRS-AP	.81	-.46	.05	.79	.52	-.07	.84	.42	.08	.79	-.48	.17
YRS-VS	.70	-.39	.42	.70	.43	.34	.74	.21	.44	.54	-.30	.56
PBI-AM	.75	-.36	-.11	.77	.48	-.25	.84	.39	.08	.75	-.52	.09
EIGENVALUES	3.75	1.03	0.78	4.29	1.33	0.78	4.20	1.32	0.87	3.67	1.39	1.06
CUMULATIVE % VARIANCE	53.6	68.3	79.4	53.7	70.2	80.0	52.5	69.1	80.0	45.9	63.2	76.4

B. *Three-Factor Varimax Rotation*[1]

VARIABLE	SKG			S1G			S2G			S3G		
	F1	F2	F3	F1	F2	F3	F1	F2	F3	F1	F2	F3
ITPA-TOTAL	.19	.69	.40	.19	.75	.31	.10	.82	.30	.33	.76	.06
PPVT	.19	.89	-.07	.13	.90	.06	.22	.85	-.11	.08	.86	.21
BINET	.28	.79	.27	.23	.78	.40	.26	.70	.47	.55	.70	.09
LEITER	.18	.22	.89	.12	.24	.86	.22	.16	.87	.80	.17	.10
CAT-TOTAL	—	—	—	.42	.29	.70	.69	.15	.46	.80	.15	.29
YRS-AP	.86	.20	.32	.90	.14	.26	.89	.12	.25	.36	.10	.86
YRS-VS	.86	.28	.07	.84	.27	-.05	.82	.33	-.10	-.10	.26	.78
PBI-AM	.70	.18	.43	.84	.11	.34	.88	.14	.25	.47	-.01	.79

[1]Shaded areas identify variables which most clearly define each factor as judged by the relative magnitude of factor loadings.

Table A-7 (continued)

C. *Two-Factor Varimax Rotation*[1]

VARIABLE	SKG		S1G		S2G		S3G	
	F1	F2	F1	F2	F1	F2	F1	F2
ITPA-TOTAL	.28	.77	.80	.21	.15	.86	.14	.82
PPVT	.14	.84	.82	.07	.14	.78	.06	.74
BINET	.32	.82	.87	.26	.36	.79	.27	.84
LEITER	.46	.44	.60	.31	.47	.37	.46	.45
CAT-TOTAL			.55	.56	.80	.24	.63	.41
YRS-AP	.91	.23	.21	.92	.92	.14	.91	.14
YRS-VS	.77	.20	.20	.79	.73	.26	.60	.12
PBI-AM	.79	.25	.22	.88	.91	.17	.91	.08

[1]Shaded areas identify variables which most clearly define each factor as judged by the relative magnitude of factor loadings.

Table A-8

*Description of Items from Factors I and II
of the Cognitive Home Environment Scale*

Factor I, Home as Learning Environment:

- Nonschool trips to other towns by child
- Availability of newspapers and magazines in home
- Availability of dictionary, encyclopedia, and library card in home
- Availability of "play" materials such as paper, scissors, crayons, etc. for use by child in home
- Purchase of "educational" gifts for child by parents

Factor II, Parent as Teacher:

- Parent reads to child
- Parent suggests that child view educational television programs
- Parent teaches new words to child
- Parent is concerned about child's speech and attempts to improve it
- Parent values and rewards intellectual accomplishments

able factor solution. Factor I was interpreted as a general measure of "Home as Learning Environment"; Factor II, as a measure of "Parent as Teacher". Factor scores were obtained by averaging the scores of items associated with each factor. Higher scores are presumed to indicate more developmentally supportive home environments.

Although the revised CHES produced more credible and more intelligible measures of home environment than its predecessor, estimates of internal reliability were not impressive. Alpha coefficients for Factors I and II were .57 and .53, respectively. In spite of their limited reliability, however, both CHES factors were incorporated in the analytic design in lieu of any better measures of the child's proximal environment. Intercorrelations of CHES factors with other measures are presented in the *Statistical Supplement*, Part B, Tables 21-30, 37, and 38.

MAI

The Maternal Attitude Inventory (MAI) represents a refinement of the Inventory of Attitudes on Family Life and Children, which was used as an independent measure of maternal attitudes in the 1970 Perry Report. The original Inventory had, in turn, been adapted from the Parental Attitude Research Instrument (Schaefer and Bell, 1958). Over the course of the project, several different versions of the instrument were administered to mothers at both FEY and SEY data collection points. Although designed to be a questionnaire, questions were read and, if necessary, explained in a standardized manner to each project mother. All items were statements with which mothers were asked if they "agreed strongly", agreed mildly", "disagreed mildly", or "disagreed strongly". In addition to data collected on mothers of children in the project sample, data were also obtained in 1962 from mothers of children who had just entered kindergarten at an all-white elementary school located in a middle-class residential area of Ypsilanti.[10]

The MAI was specifically constructed to reliably differentiate mothers with middle-class childrearing attitudes from mothers with nonmiddle-class attitudes. Data obtained from experimental-group mothers were not utilized in constructing the MAI since it was hypothesized that the childrearing attitudes of experimental mothers might have been influenced by the home teaching program which had already begun by the time data were collected. Four steps were involved in the selection of items from the total pool of items for which data had been obtained from all control group (N=60) mothers at FEY and SEY. First, items were eliminated from further consideration if there was less than a 30% difference in rates of endorsement by project and middle-class mothers. Second, of remaining items only those with test-retest (FEY/ SEY) correlation coefficients greater than .40 were retained. Third, of these items only those on which the mean score of control-group mothers changed less than one half point from FEY to SEY were retained. Finally, items still included after step three were subjected to a principal compo-

---

[10]This was roughly the same sample which provided comparison demographic data reported in chapter I, Table 3.

nent factor analysis, and items with loadings less than .45 on the first factor were eliminated. Items which met all of these criteria were subsequently incorporated in the MAI measure; they are presented in Table A-9. MAI total scores were obtained by multiplying actual item scores by the loadings of each item on the first factor from the principal component analysis, then computing the mean weighted-item score for each mother. Higher scores indicate more "middle class" attitudes.

Internal reliabilities computed at FEY and SEY for the total project sample (experimental and control) using coefficient alpha were .79 and .87, respectively. Test-retest reliability was assessed by correlating FEY with SEY MAI total scores for control-group mothers only; a correlation coefficient of .85 was obtained. Intercorrelations of MAI scores with other measures are presented in the *Statistical Supplement*, Part B, Tables 21-30, 37, and 38. It is important to note that MAI data at FEY were collected up to three months after project enrollment (post FEY, Table A-3). Since experimental-group mothers were already participating in the parent program at this point (having received up to 10 one-hour visits), the FEY MAI cannot be considered a true pre-measure independent of the experimental treatment.

Table A-9

Maternal Attitude Inventory Items

- Children should never learn things outside the home which make them doubt their parent's ideas.
- A mother should do her best to avoid any disappointment to her child.
- Parents should know better than to allow their children to be exposed to difficult situations.
- A good mother will find enough social life within the family.
- Mothers sacrifice almost all their own fun for their children.
- The trouble with giving attention to children's problems is they usually just make up a lot of stories to keep you interested.
- A mother has a right to know everything going on in her child's life because her child is part of her.
- A child soon learns that there is no greater wisdom than that of his parents.
- Some children are just so bad they must be taught to fear adults for their own good.
- There is usually something wrong with a child who asks a lot of questions about sex.

Measures of socio-emotional development

Six measures of socio-emotional development were drawn from the two teacher rating scales (YRS and PBI) already described:

- PBI Classroom Conduct Factor (PBI-CC)
- PBI Socio-Emotional State Factor (PBI-SES)
- PBI Teacher Dependence Factor (PBI-TD)

- PBI Personal Behavior Factor (PBI-PB)
- YRS Social Development Factor (YRS-SD)
- YRS Emotional Adjustment Factor (YRS-EA)

The items associated with each of these factors are presented in Table A-10. The intercorrelations of factor ratings made by different teachers over one-year intervals are presented in Table A-11. The most consistently significant correlations were found for the PBI-CC and PBI-PB factors which ostensibly measure the social acceptability of children's behavior in the classroom. The more global measures of socio-emotional adjustment were less stable.

Measures of school success

A primary objective of the experimental preschool program was that children be more successful in school. Measures of academic potential and socio-emotional development may be indicators of how well children are likely to do in school, but they are not the criterion itself. For the "high risk" children in the project sample, succeeding in school meant remaining on grade and in regular classrooms (versus retained in grade and/or placed in special education programs).

Data were collected from public school records classifying each child in the project sample into one of three categories at S1G through S4G:

- on grade, regular classroom (coded 3)
- retained in grade, regular classroom (coded 2)
- placed in special education program (coded 1)

The special education category included children placed in both integrated and self-contained programs.[11] Although self-contained programs probably have somewhat more negative implications for the social adjustment of children than integrated programs, placement in one or the other program was not a reliable indicator of the severity of a child's problem since not all school systems had both types of programs. This, in conjunction with the fact that the costs of the two programs are virtually the same, seemed to justify collapsing the categories. Retention in grade was judged to have less severe implications for the child's later adjustment and to indicate a lower level of maladjustment to the school environment than special education placement. No children in the project sample were retained in grade more than one year though some children who were retained in kindergarten, first, or second grades were later placed in special education programs. Once a child had been retained, he was classified "retained" in subsequent years unless his status changed as a result of special education placement or skipping a grade. The school

---

[11]In integrated programs, children attend both regular and special classes. Integrated special education programs may be graded or ungraded depending upon the school district. In self-contained programs, children attend only special education classes which are ungraded.

Table A-10

Items from PBI and YRS Factors
Used as Measures of Socio-Emotional Development

PUPIL BEHAVIOR INVENTORY: Classroom Conduct Factor (CC)

- Blames others for trouble
- Resistant to teacher
- Attempts to manipulate adults
- Influences others toward troublemaking
- Impulsive
- Requires continuous supervision
- Aggressive toward peers
- Disobedient
- Easily lead into trouble
- Resentful of criticism or discipline
- Disrupts classroom procedures
- Teases or provokes students

PUPIL BEHAVIOR INVENTORY: Socio-Emotional State Factor (SES)

- Appears depressed
- Withdrawn and uncommunicative
- Friendly, and well-received by other pupils
- Appears generally happy
- Isolated, few or no friends

PUPIL BEHAVIOR INVENTORY: Teacher Dependence Factor (TD)

- Seeks constant reassurance
- Possessive of teacher

PUPIL BEHAVIOR INVENTORY: Personal Behavior Factor (BP)

- Absences or truancies
- Inappropriate personal appearance
- Lying or cheating
- Steals
- Swears or uses obscene words
- Poor personal hygiene

YPSILANTI RATING SCALE: Social Development Factor (SD)

- Social relationship with classmates
- Social relationship with teacher
- Level of curiosity shown

YPSILANTI RATING SCALE: Emotional Adjustment Factor (EA)

- Level of emotional adjustment
- Degree of trust in total environment

Table A-11

Test-Retest Reliability of Elementary School Measures for the Perry Sample

Measures of Socio-Emotional Development

ONE-YEAR TEST-RETEST INTERVALS

Instrument	Experimental Group					Control Group				
	(S2Y)—SKG	SKG—S1G	S1G—S2G	S2G—S3G	S3G—S4G	(S2Y)—SKG	SKG—S1G	S1G—S2G	S2G—S3G	S3G—S4G
PBI-CC	—	.46*	.33*	.60*	—	—	.59*	.53*	.34	—
PBI-SES	—	.04	.28	.50*	—	—	.37*	.46*	.59*	—
PBI-TD	—	.17	.32*	.24	—	—	.23	.25	.49	—
PBI-PB	—	.46*	.41*	.53*	—	—	.40*	.64*	.40*	—
YRS-SD	—	.16	.33*	.19	—	—	.45*	.67*	.26	—
YRS-EA	—	-.07	.32	.45*	—	—	.39*	.56*	.20	—

Asterisks indicate significance level (*p<.10; **p<.05; ***p<.01). If no asterisks appear, the difference is not significant at or beyond the .10 level.

success measure is a meaningful ordinal scale, higher scores indicating greater success in school and less cost to the school system.

The correlations between actual success in school (i.e., grade and class placement) and concurrent measures of academic potential and socio-emotional development are presented in Table A-12.[12] School Success correlated most highly with CAT-Total scores at S3G and S4G; yet even in these instances, less than 50% of the variance in School Success was explained. Other correlations are weak (less than 9% of variance explained) to moderate (less than 2.5% of variance explained). The near absence of significant (p<.05) correlations between teacher ratings and the School Success variable is striking and misleading. Although concurrent correlations of PBI and YRS ratings with School Success are low, longitudinal correlations between earlier teacher ratings and later School Success are quite strong, indicating that teacher ratings do predict success in school (*Statistical Supplement*, Part B, Tables 35 and 36). In fact, these longitudinal correlations are comparable to or stronger than those

Table A-12

School Success Correlated with Concurrent Measures of Academic Potential and Socio-Emotional Development

Variable	CONCURRENT SCHOOL SUCCESS							
	S1G		S2G		S3G		S4G	
	EXP	CON	EXP	CON	EXP	CON	EXP	CON
A. Measures of Academic Potential								
Binet	.23	.28*	.46*	.29*	.45*	.39*	.37*	.44*
Leiter	.11	.15	.43*	.12	.35*	.39*	———	———
PPVT	.16	.22	.20	.18	.24	.27*	———	———
ITPA-Total	.25	.14	.43*	.07	.40*	.48*	———	———
ITPA-AVAS	.27*	.19	.49*	.01	.45*	.24	———	———
CAT-Total	.24	.29*	.44*	.11	.49*	.53*	.62*	.68*
PBI-AM	−.01	.07	.25	.05	.14	.24	———	———
YRS-AP	−.03	.02	.21	.18	.10	.24	———	———
YRS-VS	.20	.09	.23	.26	.23	.08	———	———
B. Measures of Socio-Emotional Adjustment								
PBI-CC	−.03	.08	.07	.03	−.11	.02	———	———
PBI-SES	.25	.08	.12	.15	.44*	.11	———	———
PBI-TD	−.02	−.10	.18	−.01	.09	−.12	———	———
PBI-PB	.07	.10	.30*	.11	.30	.17	———	———
YRS-SD	.16	.00	.19	.20	.17	.05	———	———
YRS-EA	.08	.04	.09	.13	.22	.19	———	———

*Asterisks indicate significance level (*p<.10; **p<.05; ***p<.01). If no asterisks appear, the difference is not significant at or beyond the .10 level.*

[12]The magnitudes of correlation coefficients are somewhat restricted by the distribution form of the trichotomous school success variable (the majority of children are on grade in regular classrooms at every testpoint). First- and second-grade data should be considered very cautiously, if at all, since few children were either retained or placed in special education in these grades.

between other measures and the School Success variable at or across any points in time (*Statistical Supplement*, Part B, Tables 31-36). In light of this evidence it seems likely that from S1G through S4G the behavior of children who were retained in grade or placed in special education was rated with reference to other unsuccessful children or younger children and that consequently teacher ratings for unsuccessful children were spuriously high, thereby deflating concurrent correlations of teacher ratings with the criterion. At the same time, the relatively high concurrent correlations of school success with Binet, Leiter, ITPA, and CAT at S3G and S4G may have been inflated somewhat by spuriously low scores of unsuccessful children who by virtue of their retention in grade or placement in special programs may not have had opportunities to progress as rapidly as they might have in acquiring skills fundamental to the tests cited. More important than these possibilities, however, is the finding that less than 50% of the variance in actual school success was accounted for by any other measure at any point in time. Clearly, exclusive reliance on "predictors" and "indices" of academic competency is no substitute for more direct measurement of the criterion.

Appendix B: Statistical methodology

The discussion which follows describes the ANOVA design and the regression designs used throughout this report. Broad research questions are restated as specific, testable hypotheses in terms of one or both of the analytic designs, and the procedures used to test these hypotheses are described.

Conventional analysis of variance (ANOVA)

Conventional three-way ANOVA techniques were used to replicate analyses performed in the 1970 Perry Report, this time on complete data from all waves through fourth grade (S4G).[1] The ANOVA design incorporated three factors:

- Group (Treatment Group), comparing experimental (EXP) with control (CON)
- Sex (sex of child), comparing boys with girls
- Wave (age cohort and replication sample), comparing Waves 0, 1, 2, 3, and 4

---

[1]Computations were performed using a computer program AVAR23 adapted from Veldman (1967).

In addition, the interactions of these factors were included:

- *Group* x *Sex* interaction
- *Group* x *Wave* interaction
- *Sex* x *Wave* interaction
- *Group* x *Sex* x *Wave* interaction

Six of the research questions stated in chapter II ("Overview") were addressed using this analytic design.

Analysis for Questions 1 and 9:
Benefits of the experimental treatment

It was hypothesized that children in the experimental group would evidence higher (i.e., more positive or better) scores on outcome measures than children in the control group as a result of their preschool experience and that parents of children in the experimental group would evidence more developmentally supportive attitudes and behavior than control group parents as a result of the home teaching component of the experimental treatment. These hypotheses were tested as the Group main effect on child and parent outcomes within the three-way ANOVA design. This is to say, an F test was performed to determine whether inclusion of the Treatment Group Membership variable in the ANOVA design significantly reduced the error variance (unexplained variance) in outcome measures over and above the reductions in error variance associated with other factors in the design (Sex, Wave, and the interaction terms). The significance levels reported in chapter II are for nondirectional F tests, most commonly used in presenting ANOVA findings. Although nondirectional tests are appropriate for other questions addressed using ANOVA, the Treatment Group hypothesis is clearly directional (EXP > CON). Consequently, it should be noted that nondirectional F tests for the Group main effect which reach significance at the .10 level are equivalent to directional tests at the .05 level.

Analysis for Question 3:
Differential effects of preschool on boys and girls

There was no particular expectation regarding the possibility of differential Sex effects within Treatment Groups on outcome measures except in the case of California Achievement Test scores obtained during the post-treatment period. In general, then, this question was addressed by simply testing the Group x Sex interaction, over and above other factors in the ANOVA design, against the null hypothesis. The use of planned comparisons in analyses of CAT data followed Hays (1963) and is discussed in greater detail in the section "Findings for the Post-Treatment Period" in chapter II.

Analysis for Question 4:
Differential effects of preschool by wave

The possibility that preschool might have had different effects upon experimental-group children in different waves as a result of changes in program operations was examined by testing the Group x Wave interaction over and above other factors in the ANOVA design, against the null hypothesis. There were no particular expectations regarding the direction of differences since the treatment had not been systematically manipulated. It did seem likely, however, that any interaction of Group with Wave would manifest itself as a "simple effect" (Winer, 1962) of Wave within the experimental group.

Analysis for Question 7: Overall sex differences

Again, there were no specific expectations regarding overall differences between boys and girls on outcome measures. The question of sex differences was addressed by testing the Sex main effect (i.e., the effect of Sex over and above Group, Wave, and the interactions) against the null hypothesis.

Analysis for Question 8: Overall wave differences

Although Wave was incorporated as a main effect in the ANOVA design primarily as a "blocking factor" to increase the precision of tests of other effects, the findings of overall Wave effects are examined in this report because of the implications of sampling error in small-scale experimental studies. The possibility that scores on dependent measures might vary systematically by wave (i.e., replication sample and age cohort) was examined by testing the Wave main effect over and above other main effects and interactions, against the null hypothesis.

Unexamined factors in the ANOVA design

Although Sex x Wave and Group x Sex x Wave interactions were of no particular interest in the context of this study, they were incorporated in the ANOVA design both to achieve comparability with analyses performed for the previous report and to take advantage of available computer programs which did not permit collapsing these interactions into the error term. Visual inspection of complete ANOVA results (summarized in the *Statistical Supplement*, Part A) suggests that inclusion of these two interactions may have reduced the power of other tests somewhat since the degrees of freedom (df's) sacrificed by their inclusion do not seem to have been compensated for by corresponding reductions in the error variance of dependent measures. The findings for these interactions are not considered in the text of this report.

Regression analysis

The analytic techniques described here represent an alternative to conventional analysis of variance, utilizing multiple linear regression methods rather than traditional ANOVA procedures to test experimental hypotheses (see, e.g., Cohen, 1968; McNeil, Kelly, and McNeil, 1973). In the context of this study, the major advantage of regression analysis lies in the possibility of testing main effects and interactions which incorporate both categorical (e.g., Treatment Group) and continuous variables (e.g., SES or FEY Binet scores). The relationship between the regression design described here and conventional ANOVA is discussed in Overall and Spiegel (1969; specifically "Method 2").

The questions which are addressed here were also explored in the 1970 Perry Report using stepwise regression techniques. The regression design employed in re-analysis and in extended analyses of data for this report, however, is substantially different from the previous design and more adequate for testing the specific hypotheses of interest in this study. Because of discrepancies in the analytic designs no attempt will be made to summarize the results of the previous report other than to note tentative conclusions when appropriate.

Whereas ANOVA techniques were used to analyze all pertinent dependent measures obtained on children and parents in the Perry sample, a subset of major dependent variables were used as criterion measures in regression analyses: Binet scores (FEY-S4G), CAT scores (S1G-S4G), and the School Success variable (S4G). The independent or predictor variables included in the regression design are summarized in Table B-1. Variance associated with Treatment Group Membership was removed from six post-enrollment measures prior to their inclusion as independent variables in regression analyses: FEY Leiter, FEY ITPA, FEY PPVT, FEY MAI, CHES1, and CHES2. In each case, scores were regressed on the dichotomous treatment variable (EXP/CON) and the difference between actual

Table B-1

Summary of Independent Variables Used in Regression Analyses

VARIABLE CODE	VARIABLE DESCRIPTION[1]
EXP	Experimental Group: The variable contained a 1 if the subject was a member of the experimental group; 0 if control.
CON	Control Group: The variable contained a 1 if the subject was a member of the control group; 0 if experimental.
Entering Child Characteristics	Four measures of entering child characteristics: FEY BINET FEY LEITER/R FEY ITPA/R FEY PPVT/R
Home Environment Factors	Five measures of home environment: MO. EDUC.: Mother's Education (years completed) SES: SES Rating MAI/R: Maternal Attitude Inventory (FEY) CHES1/R: Cognitive Home Environment Scale (Factor 1) CHES2/R: Cognitive Home Environment Scale (Factor 2)

[1]The suffix "/R" indicates that residual scores, independent of treatment, were used.

and predicted scores (the residual variance) saved. The net effect of these procedures was to adjust treatment group means on each variable as in analysis of covariance. The largest amount of variance (7%) was removed from FEY Leiter scores which were obtained up to three months after treatment began; the smallest amount (2%) from CHES factors.

Basic analytic procedures

Before discussing tests of specific hypotheses, a brief description of basic analytic procedures is presented for readers who are unfamiliar with the use of regression for analysis of variance.

For each specific hypothesis which is tested, *full* and *restricted* regression models (equations) are constructed. The full model reflects the hypothesized situation, and the restricted model reflects the alternative, or null, hypothesis. For example, if the hypothesis were that "there was a difference between experimental and control groups on the dependent (criterion) measure SEY Binet", the full model would contain Treatment Group Membership variables and the restricted model would not:

EXAMPLE FULL MODEL[2]: SEY Binet = $a_0U + (a_1EXP + a_2CON) + E_1$

EXAMPLE RESTRICTED MODEL: SEY Binet = $a_0U + E_1$

Using a multiple linear regression computer program[3], the amount of variance in SEY Binet explained by the predictor variables in each model is determined, the variance explained being expressed as the square multiple correlation coefficient between predictors and criterion (R^2). In the example restricted model above, R^2 equals 0.0 since the model contains no information other than the unit vector (U) which in this instance generates the grand mean. An F test for the difference in R^2 values between the two models provides a statistical comparison of their relative predictive powers.[4] If the F ratio is significant, the full model is accepted as the best model, and the null hypothesis is rejected. If the F ratio is not significant, the restricted model is accepted as the best model, and the null hypothesis is not rejected. The test described in this example is exactly equivalent to a t test for the difference between two means.

In the actual analyses reported here, independent variables were

---

[2]Definition of terms in regression equations:

U = the unit vector which has a value of 1 for each subject and generates the regression constant,

E = the error term; variance in the criterion not explained by the predictors in the model,

$a_0, a_1 \ldots a_2$ = partial regression weights calculated to minimize the error variance.

[3]The program LINEAR (Kelly, Beggs, McNeil, Eichelberger, and Lyon, 1969) was used to perform regression analyses for this report.

[4]$$F = \frac{R^2 \text{ full model} - R^2 \text{ restricted model}/df_1}{1 - R^2 \text{ full model}/df_2}$$

df_1 = the number of linearly independent variables in the full model minus the number of linearly independent variables on the restricted model

df_2 = N minus the number of linearly independent variables in the full model

grouped into three sets as indicated in Table B-1: Group (EXP and CON); Entering Child Characteristics (FEY Binet, FEY Leiter/R, FEY ITPA/R, and FEY PPVT/R); and Environmental Factors (Mother's Education, SES, FEY MAI/R, CHES1/R, and CHES2/R). The restricted models used to test Entering Child Characteristics as a predictor exclude all variables in that set, thus the test is not of predictions by individual variables (FEY Binet, FEY Leiter/R, FEY ITPA/R, FEY PPVT/R) but of their joint effect. The set of independent variables constituting Home Environment Factors was treated in the same way. While the division of independent variables into these two sets has considerable face validity, it is also supported by the results of a principal component analysis performed on all independent variables except Group. Two components with eigenvalues greater than 1.0 were extracted. Following a Varimax rotation of these factors, variables in the Entering Child Characteristics set loaded strongly on one factor and variables in the Home Environment Factors set loaded strongly on the other. The full sets of variables, rather than factor scores, were used in order to avoid any loss of information.

Analysis for Question 1:
Benefits of the experimental treatment

It was hypothesized that children in the experimental group would score higher than children in the control group on criterion measures with certain entering characteristics of children (Entering Child Characteristics, Table B-1) and background factors (Home Environment Factors, Table B-1) statistically controlled (i.e., incorporated as covariates in the regression design). This hypothesis is related to, but importantly different from, the hypothesis of a Group main effect within the three-way ANOVA design already described where the Group effect was tested with Sex, Wave, and the interactions of the three Main Effects statistically controlled. The regression design used to test this hypothesis is equivalent to a conventional one-way analysis of covariance, testing the Group main effect while covarying on nine continuous variables. The full regression model reflecting this hypothesis—"Full Model for Main Effects"—is presented in Table B-2. It contains three sets of predictor variables: Treatment Group, Entering Child Characteristics, and Home Environment Factors (the latter two being the covariates).[5] The restricted model used to test this hypothesis—Restricted Model A—does not contain Group as a predictor but does retain the covariates (Table B-2). A directional F test was used to test the hypothesis: EXP>CON (F test on the difference between R_f^2 and R_r^2).

Analysis for Question 2:
Relative importance of group versus other predictors

The relative importance of Group, Entering Child Characteristics, and Home Environment Factors as predictors of criterion measures was also

---

[5]More detailed descriptions of all models used in the analyses reported here are presented in the *Statistical Supplement*, Part C.

Table B-2

Specification of Full and Restricted Regression Models for Testing the Main Effects of Treatment Group, Entering Child Characteristics, and Home Environment Factors[1]

REGRESSION MODELS	Number of linearly independent variables	df for this model tested against full model
FULL MODEL FOR MAIN EFFECTS: CRITERION = EXP + CON + Child Characteristics + Environmental Factors MEASURE	11	
RESTRICTED MODEL A (testing main effect of Treatment Group): CRITERION = Child Characteristics + Environmental Factors MEASURE	10	1/N-11
RESTRICTED MODEL B (testing main effect of entering Child Characteristics): CRITERION = EXP + CON + Environmental Factors MEASURE	7	4/N-11
RESTRICTED MODEL C (testing main effect of Environmental Factors): CRITERION = EXP + CON + Child Characteristics MEASURE	6	5/N-11

[1]For simplicity of presentation, the unit vector (U), the error term (E), and the regression constants (a_i) are excluded and the actual variables which make up the entering child characteristics and home environment factors are not specified in these models. The complete models are found in the *Statistical Supplement*, Table C-3.

examined using regression techniques. There was no particular expectation regarding the differential predictive power of these variables. The full model remained the same as that used for testing the Group main effect (Full Model for Main Effects, Table B-2). Three restricted models (A, B, and C in Table B-2) were used to test the unique contribution of each of the three predictors. Each test involved eliminating one component from the full model (the one being tested) in order to determine the proportion of variance which could be accounted for without that predictor.[6] The difference between the R^2 value for each of these restricted models (R^2_r a, b, c) and the R^2 value of the full model (R^2_f) indicates the unique contribution of the component (Main Effects variable set) left out of each restricted model. These "decreases in R^2" can then be compared to determine the relative contributions of each predictor variable set. Nondirectional F tests were used to test the main effects of Entering Child Characteristics and Home Environment Factors.

It should be noted that in the analyses reported here not all of the variance explained by the joint effect (R^2_f) of the predictor variables can be uniquely attributed to individual predictors. The reason that R^2's from the restricted models do not sum to the R^2 obtained in the full model is because part of the variance in the criterion measures explained by the predictor variables is overlapping. This is to say, the predictors are not only correlated with the criterion but, in some degree, with one another. The intercorrelations of predictors (the components of predictor variable sets) with one another and their bivariate correlations with criterion measures for the preschool and post-treatment periods are presented in Tables B-3 through B-6 in order to give the reader some idea of the complex interdependencies of variables in the regression analyses.

Analyses for Questions 5 & 6:
Differential effects of entering levels of academic potential and home environment factors within the experimental and control groups

Since bivariate correlations between individual predictor variables and criterion measures were positive (or zero) within both treatment groups (Tables B-5 and B-6), it was evident that the joint effects of these variables as Entering Child Characteristics (entering measures of academic potential) and Home Environment Factors would also be positive in both groups. Specifically it was hypothesized that the effect of Home Environment Factors would be strongest in the control group and the overall interaction of Group with Home Environment Factors, statistically significant (directional F test). This pattern of effects was suggested by tentative findings presented in the 1970 Perry Report. There were no particular expectations regarding the possibility of differential effects of Entering Child Characteristics within the experimental and control groups. Consequently, a nondirectional test of the Group x Entering Child Characteristics interaction against the null hypothesis was performed.

---

[6] Two-tailed F tests were used to test the main effects of Entering Child Characteristics and Home Environment Factors.

Table B-3

Intercorrelation of Measures Used as Independent Variables in Regression Analyses by Treatment Groups[1]

A. Experimental Group (N = 48)

VARIABLE	MO. EDUC.	SES	FEY MAI/R	CHES1/R	CHES2/R	FEY BINET	FEY LEITER/R	FEY ITPA/R	FEY PPVT/R
MO. EDUC.	1.00								
SES	.72*	1.00							
FEY MAI/R	.32*	.21	1.00						
CHES1/R	.51*	.36*	.10	1.00					
CHES2/R	.29*	.42*	.07	.18	1.00				
FEY BINET	.19	.23	.19	.20	-.06	1.00			
FEY LEITER/R	.16	.12	.02	.18	.15	.22	1.00		
FEY ITPA/R	.11	.21	-.20	.31*	.08	.29*	.52*	1.00	
FEY PPVT/R	.15	.22	.04	.21	.02	.48*	.21	.38*	1.00

B. Control Group (N = 50)

VARIABLE	MO. EDUC.	SES	FEY MAI/R	CHES1/R	CHES2/R	FEY BINET	FEY LEITER/R	FEY ITPA/R	FEY PPVT/R
MO. EDUC.	1.00								
SES	.76*	1.00							
FEY MAI/R	.36*	.34*	1.00						
CHES1/R	.24	.28	.09	1.00					
CHES2/R	.27	.31*	.10	.14	1.00				
FEY BINET	.16	.20	.02	.07	-.23	1.00			
FEY LEITER/R	.26	.34*	.21	.25	-.02	.37*	1.00		
FEY ITPA/R	.16	.08	.10	.18	-.10	.12	.23	1.00	
FEY PPVT/R	.10	.11	.22	.18	.20	.35*	.39*	.00	1.00

[1]Correlations are based on the total regression subsample: children with complete data on all independent variables. In the regression analyses considered in this volume the subsamples actually used are often smaller due to missing data on the criterion measures.

Asterisks indicate significance level (*p<.10; **p<.05; ***p<.01). If no asterisks appear, the difference is not significant at or beyond the .10 level.

Table B-4

Product-Moment Correlations Between
Independent Variables and Criterion Measures
Used in Regression Analyses: Preschool Period[1]

VARIABLES	SEY BINET			S2Y BINET		
	TOTAL SAMPLE	EXP	CON	TOTAL SAMPLE	EXP	CON
GROUP[2]	−.52*	——	——	−.45*	——	——
MO. EDUC.	.29*	.40*	.23	.16	.14	.28
SES	.35*	.43*	.34*	.26*	.22	.34*
FEY MAI/R	.17	.17	.22	.07	.02	.08
CHES1/R	.15	.17	.23	.17	.20	.38*
CHES2/R	−.07	−.02	−.12	.07	.16	.06
FEY BINET	.47*	.57*	.47*	.35*	.35*	.40*
FEY LEITER/R	.25*	.29*	.31*	.30*	.35*	.41*
FEY ITPA/R	.16	.10	.19	.20	.38*	.17
FEY PPVT/R	.30*	.31*	.36*	.19	.16	.34*

[1]Correlations are based on the same subsamples as regression analyses.
[2]GROUP: 1 = EXP; 2 = CON

*Asterisks indicate significance level (*p<.10; **p<.05; ***p<.01). If no asterisks appear, the difference is not significant at or beyond the .10 level.*

The full regression model for testing these interactions was obtained by adding the interaction variables to the "Full Model for Main Effects" described in Table B-2. There is no direct analog for this design in conventional analysis of variance since the interactions incorporate both categorical (Group) and continuous variables (Entering Child Characteristics and Home Environment Factors). The full and restricted models used to test the interactions are described in Table B-7. Restricted Model D contains the main effects of Group and Entering Child Characteristics along with the Group x Home Environment Factors interaction variables. This model, tested against the Full Model for Interactions containing the Group x Entering Child Characteristics interaction variables, provided the test of signficance for the interaction between Group and Entering Child Characteristics over and above the interaction of Group with Home Environment Factors and the Group and Entering Child Characteristics main effects. Restricted Model E contains the main effect of Home Environment Factors, and the Group main effect and the interaction of Group with Entering Child Characteristics. This model, tested against the Full Model for Interactions, provided the test of significance for the interaction of Group with Home Environment Factors over and above the Group x Entering Child Characteristics interaction and the Home Environment Factors and Group main effects.

When a significant interaction was found, it was necessary to determine for which group the effect was strongest. This was done by testing for simple effects within each group using restricted models F through I (Table B-7). In models F and G, the interaction between Group and Entering Child Characteristics was dropped out for the experimental group and then for the control group. The magnitude of decrease in R^2 from full to

Table B-5

Product-Moment Correlations Between Independent Variables and Criterion Measures Used in Regression Analyses: Elementary School Period[1]

A. Binet as Criterion

VARIABLES	SKG Total Sample	SKG EXP	SKG CON	S1G Total Sample	S1G EXP	S1G CON	S2G Total Sample	S2G EXP	S2G CON	S3G Total Sample	S3G EXP	S3G CON	S4G Total Sample	S4G EXP	S4G CON
GROUP[2]	-.23	—	—	-.22*	—	—	-.04	—	—	-.03	—	—	.00	—	—
MO. EDUC.	.27*	.23	.34*	.24*	.27	.20	.34*	.31*	.38*	.22*	.30*	.14	.37*	.27	.49*
SES	.39*	.37*	.42*	.40*	.48*	.30*	.38*	.37*	.41*	.38*	.38*	.38*	.37*	.29*	.45*
FEY MAI/R	.15	.00	.32*	.10	.03	.18	.15	.12	.20	.13	.06	.17	.23*	.18	.28
CHES1/R	.17	.20	.15	.22*	.24	.21	.19	.25	.10	.27*	.26	.31	.27*	.32*	.22
CHES2/R	.10	.15	.04	.02	.15	-.10	.01	.10	-.08	.09	.23	-.01	.04	.12	-.03
FEY BINET	.50*	.54*	.48*	.45*	.49*	.42*	.42*	.65*	.19	.44*	.50*	.39*	.34*	.35*	.34*
FEY LEITER/R	.36*	.35*	.41*	.33*	.34*	.33*	.36*	.38*	.32*	.50*	.56*	.46*	.38*	.37*	.41*
FEY ITPA/R	.18	.20	.14	.26*	.30*	.21	.22*	.31*	.09	.34*	.41*	.28	.30*	.34*	.26
FEY PPVT/R	.36*	.28	.52*	.28*	.27	.29*	.22*	.23	.21	.31*	.34*	.31*	.26*	.29*	.23

B. CAT as Criterion

VARIABLES	S1G Total Sample	S1G EXP	S1G CON	S2G Total Sample	S2G EXP	S2G CON	S3G Total Sample	S3G EXP	S3G CON	S4G Total Sample	S4G EXP	S4G CON
GROUP[2]	-.16	—	—	-.18	—	—	-.15	—	—	-.12	—	—
MO. EDUC.	.47*	.44*	.51*	.46*	.37*	.53*	.43*	.37*	.50*	.42*	.50*	.35*
SES	.47*	.44*	.50*	.44*	.40*	.46*	.45*	.35*	.54*	.40*	.38*	.42*
FEY MAI/R	.25*	.24	.28	.21	-.04	.40*	.17	-.12	.44*	.32*	.13	.50*
CHES1/R	.29*	.19	.45*	.39*	.55*	.23	.38*	.45*	.33*	.43*	.43*	.47*
CHES2/R	.12	.12	.11	.17	.18	.18	.21	.26	.16	.11	.08	.14
FEY BINET	.40*	.51*	.31*	.29*	.38*	.20	.22*	.17	.26	.24*	.33*	.17
FEY LEITER/R	.37*	.39*	.34*	.29*	.29	.29	.36*	.42*	.31	.34*	.40*	.27
FEY ITPA/R	.14	.22	.02	.19	.31*	.04	.19	.28	.10	.14	.25	.00
FEY PPVT/R	.40*	.38*	.43*	.27*	.25*	.31*	.29*	.30*	.31	.26*	.27	.29

[1] Correlations are based on the same subsamples as regression analyses.

[2] GROUP: 1 = EXP; 2 = CON

Asterisks indicate significance level (*p<.10; **p<.05; ***p<.01). If no asterisks appear, the difference is not significant at or beyond the .10 level.

restricted models was used as an indication of the relative magnitude of effects in the two groups. Restricted models H and I were used in the same way to determine for which group the effect of Home Environment Factors was strongest. For example, if the decrease in R^2 from the Full Model for Interactions to the restricted models was greater for Restricted Model I than for Model H, the effect of Home Environment Factors would be strongest for the control group.

Table B-6

Product-Moment Correlations of
Independent Variables Used in Regression Analyses
with School Success[1]

VARIABLES	SCHOOL SUCCESS S4G		
	TOTAL SAMPLE	EXP	CON
GROUP[2]	−.20*	——	——
MO. EDUC.	.29*	.39*	.22
SES	.31*	.31*	.31*
FEY MAI/R	.18	−.11	.40*
CHES1/R	.19	.22	.18
CHES2/R	−.01	−.01	.00
FEY BINET	.27*	.40*	.18
FEY LEITER/R	.26*	.34*	.19
FEY ITPA/R	.18	.27	.09
FEY PPVT/R	.33	.31*	.40*

[1]Correlations are based on the same subsamples as regression analyses.

[2]GROUP: 1 = EXP;   2 = CON

Asterisks indicate significance level (*p<.10; **p<.05; ***p<.01).
If no asterisks appear, the difference is not significant at or beyond the .10 level.

Table B-7

Specification of Full and Restricted Regression Models for Testing Interactions Between Group and Entering Child Characteristics (CHILD) and Between Group and Home Environment Factors (ENV) [1]

MODELS	Number of linearly independent variables	df for this model tested against full model
FULL MODEL FOR INTERACTIONS (contains group main effects and all interactions):		
CRITERION MEASURE = EXP + CON + (EXP*CHILD) + (CON*CHILD) + (EXP*ENV) + (CON*ENV)	20	——[†]
RESTRICTED MODEL D (testing for interaction of Group x Child Characteristics):		
CRITERION MEASURE = EXP + CON + Child Characteristics + (EXP*ENV) + (CON*ENV)	16	4/N-20
RESTRICTED MODEL E (testing for interaction of Group x Environmental Factors):		
CRITERION MEASURE = EXP + CON + (EXP*CHILD) + (CON*CHILD) + Environmental Factors	15	5/N-20
RESTRICTED MODEL F (determining the magnitude of the effect of Child Characteristics within the EXP group):		
CRITERION MEASURE = EXP + CON + (CON*CHILD) + (EXP*ENV) + (CON*ENV)	16	——[†]
RESTRICTED MODEL G (determining the magnitude of the effect of Child Characteristics within the CON group):		
CRITERION MEASURE = EXP + CON + (EXP*CHILD) + (EXP*ENV) + (CON*ENV)	16	——[†]
RESTRICTED MODEL H (determining the magnitude of the effect of Environmental Factors within the EXP group):		
CRITERION MEASURE = EXP + CON + (EXP*CHILD) + (CON*CHILD) + (CON*ENV)	15	——[†]
RESTRICTED MODEL I (determining the magnitude of the effect of Environmental Factors within the CON group):		
CRITERION MEASURE = EXP + CON + (EXP*CHILD) + (CON*CHILD) + (EXP*ENV)	15	——[†]

[1]For simplicity of presentation, the unit vector (U), the error term (E), and the regression constants (a_i) are excluded and the actual variables which make up the child characteristics and environmental factors are not specified in these models. The complete models are found in the *Statistical Supplement*, Table C-3.

[†]No test was performed.

References

Arthur, G. *The Arthur Adaptation of the Leiter International Performance Scale, the Psychological Service Center Press.* Beverly Hills, Cal.: Western Psychological Services, 1952.

Beller, E.K. The evaluation of effects of early educational intervention on intellectual and social development of lower-class disadvantaged children. In E. Grotberg (Ed.), *Critical issues in research related to disadvantaged children.* Princeton, N.J.: Educational Testing Service, 1969.

Bennett, N., Jordan, J., Long, G., & Wade, B. *Teaching styles and pupil progress.* London, England: Open Books Publishing Limited, 1976.

Bensberg, G.J., & Sloan, W. Performance of brain-injured defectives on the Arthur Adaptation of the Leiter. *Psychological Services Center Journal,* 1951, *3,* 181-4.

Beverly, L., & Bensberg, G.J. A comparison of the Leiter International Performance Scale. *Journal of Consulting Psychology,* 1950, *14,* 234.

Blalock, H.M. *Social statistics.* New York: McGraw-Hill Book Company, 1960.

Cicirelli, V., Cooper, W., & Granger, R. *The impact of Head Start: An evaluation of the effects of the Head Start experience on children's cognitive and affective development.* Athens, Ohio: Westinghouse Learning Corporation and Ohio University, 1969.

Cohen, J. Multiple regression as a general data-analytic system. *Psychological Bulletin,* 1968, *70* (6), 423-426.

Dave, R.H. *The identification and measurement of environmental process variables that are related to educational achievement.* Unpublished doctoral dissertation, The University of Chicago, 1963.

Deutsch, M. *The Institute for Developmental Studies annual report and descriptive statement.* New York: New York University, 1962.

Di Lorenzo, L.T., Salter, R., & Brady, J.J. *Prekindergarten programs for educationally disadvantaged children.* Albany: University of the State of New York, 1969.

Dunn, L.M. *Peabody Picture Vocabulary Test manual.* Minneapolis, Minn.: American Guidance Service, 1965.

Flavell, J.H. *The developmental psychology of Jean Piaget.* New York: Van Nostrand Reinhold Company, 1963.

Fox, D.J., & Guire, K.E. *Michigan interactive data analysis systems* (2nd ed.). Ann Arbor: The University of Michigan, Statistical Research Laboratory, 1973.

Fuller, E. *Values in early childhood education.* Washington, D.C.: National Education Association, 1960.

Gray, S.W., & Klaus, R.A. The early training project: A seventh year report. *Child Development,* 1970, *41* (4), 909-924.

Gretzler, A. *The use of the Arthur Adaptation of the Leiter International Performance Scale as compared with the Stanford-Binet in diagnosing children with central nervous system disfunctioning.* Unpublished doctoral dissertation, University of Michigan, 1973.

Hays, W.L. *Statistics for psychologists.* New York: Holt, Rinehart and Winston, 1963.

Hohmann, M., Banet, B., & Weikart, D.P. *Young children in action: A manual for preschool educators.* Ypsilanti, Mich.: High/Scope Educational Research Foundation, 1978.

Hunt, J.McV. *Intelligence and experience.* New York: Ronald Press, 1961.

Jencks, C., Smith, M., Acland, H., Bane, M., Cohen, D., Gentis, H., Heyns, B., & Michelson, S. *Inequality: A reassessment of the effect of family and schooling in America.* New York: Basic Books, 1972.

Jersild, A.T., & Fite, M.D. The influence of nursery school experience on children's social adjustments. *Monographs of the Society for Research in Child Development,* 1939, *2.*

Jorgenson, C.C. IQ tests and their educational supporters. *Journal of Social Issues,* 1973, *29* (1), 36-39.

Karnes, M.B. Evaluation and implications of research with young handicapped and low-income children. In J.C. Stanley (Ed.), *Compensatory education for children, ages 2 to 8.* Baltimore, Md.: Johns Hopkins University Press, 1973.

Kellaghan, T. *The evaluation of a preschool programme for disadvantaged children.* Atlantic Highlands, N.J.: Humanities Press, Inc., 1977.

Kelly, F.J., Beggs, D.L., McNeil, K.A., Eichelberger, T., & Lyon, J. *Research design in the behavioral sciences: Multiple regression approach.* Carbondale: Southern Illinois University Press, 1969.

Kirk, S.A. *Early education of the mentally retarded.* Urbana: University of Illinois Press, 1958.

Lambie, D.Z., Bond, J.T., & Weikart, D.P. Home teaching with mothers and infants, the Ypsilanti-Carnegie Infant Education Project: An experiment. *Monographs of the High/Scope Educational Research Foundation,* 1974, No.2.

Leventhal, D.S., & Stedman, D.J. *A factor analytic study of the performance of 340 disadvantaged children on the Illinois Test of Psycholinguistic Abilities.* Unpublished manuscript, Department of Psychiatry, Duke University and the Education Improvement Program, 1967.

McCarthy, J.J., & Kirk, S.A. *Examiner's manual: Illinois Test of Psycholinguistic Abilities, experimental version.* Urbana: University of Illinois, Institute for Research on Exceptional Children, 1961.

McCarthy, J.J., & Kirk, S.A. *The construction, standardization and statistical characteristics of the Illinois Test of Psycholinguistic Abilities.* Madison, Wis.: Photo Press, 1963.

McClelland, D. Testing for competence rather than for intelligence. *American Psychologist,* January 1973.

McNeil, K.A., Kelly, F.J., & McNeil, J.T. *Testing research hypotheses using multiple linear regression.* Carbondale, Ill.: Author, 1973.

Meier, D. *Reading failure and the tests.* An occasional paper of the Workshop Center for Open Education, February 1973.

Mercer, J.R. Pluralistic diagnosis in the evaluation of Black and Chicano children: A procedure for taking social variables into account in clinical assessment. *California School Psychology,* 1971, 19(1), 23-27.

Miller, B., & Dyer, J. Four preschool programs: Their dimensions and effects. *Monographs of the Society for Research in Child Development,* 1975, 40(1962), 5-6.

Myers, J.L. *Fundamentals of experimental design.* Boston, Mass.: Allyn and Bacon, Inc., 1972.

Orgel, A.M., & Dreger, R.M. Comparative study of the Arthur-Leiter and Stanford-Binet Intelligence Scales. *Journal of Genetic Psychology,* 1955, 86, 359-365.

Overall, J.E., & Spiegel, D.K. Concerning least squares analysis of experimental data. *Psychological Bulletin,* 1969, 72(5), 311-322.

Palmer, F.H. *The effects of minimal early intervention on subsequent IQ scores and reading achievement, final report for Education Commission of the States.* Stony Brook: State University of New York, 1976.

Schaefer, E.S., & Bell, R.Q. Development of a parental attitude research instrument. *Child Development,* 1958, 29, 339-361.

Schweinhart, L.J., & Weikart, D.P. Research report—Can preschool education make a lasting difference? *Bulletin of the High/Scope Foundation,* Fall 1977, No. 4.

Scott, J.P. Critical periods in behavioral development. *Science,* 1962, 138(3544).

Seitz, V., Apfel, N.H., & Efron, C. *Long-term effects of intervention: A longitudinal investigation.* Connecticut: Hamden-New Haven Cooperative Education Center, 1976.

Skeels, H.M., Updegraff, R., Wellman, B.L., & Williams, H.M. A study of environmental stimulation: An orphanage preschool project. *University of Iowa Studies in Child Welfare,* 1938, 15, 7-191.

Skodak, M., & Skeels, H.M. A final follow-up study of one hundred adopted children. *Journal of Genetic Psychology,* 1949, 75, 85-125.

Smith, G., & James, T. The effects of preschool education: Some American and British evidence. *Oxford Review of Education,* 1(3), 1975, 223-240.

Smith, M.S. *Some short-term effects of project Head Start: A preliminary report on the second year of planned variation—1970-71.* Cambridge, Mass.: Huron Institute, 1973.

Stallings, J. Implementation and child effects of teaching practices in Follow Through classrooms. *Monographs of the Society for Research in Child Development,* 1975, 40 (7-8, Serial No. 163).

Tate, M.E. The influence of cultural factors on the Leiter International Performance Scale. *Journal of Abnormal and Social Psychology*, 1952, *47*, 497-501.

Terman, L.M., & Merrill, M.A. *Stanford-Binet Intelligence Scale, Form L-M: Manual for the third revision.* Boston, Mass.: Houghton Mifflin, 1960.

Tiegs, E.W., & Clark, W.W. *Manual: California Achievement Test, complete battery (lower primary).* Monterey Park: California Test Bureau (McGraw-Hill), 1957a.

Tiegs, E.W., & Clark, W.W. *Manual: California Achievement Test, complete battery (upper primary).* Monterey Park: California Test Bureau (McGraw-Hill), 1957b.

Vaughan, G.M., & Corballis, M.C. Beyond tests of significance: Estimating strength of effects in selected ANOVA designs. *Psychological Bulletin*, 1969, *72*(3), 204-213.

Veldman, D.J. *Fortran programming for the behavioral sciences.* New York: Holt, Rinehart and Winston, 1967.

Vinter, R.D., Sarri, R.C., Vorwaller, D.J., & Schafer, W.E. *Pupil Behavior Inventory: A manual of administration and scoring.* Ann Arbor, Mich.: Campus Publishers, 1966.

Waddel, K.J., & Cahoon, D.D. Comments on the use of the Illinois Test of Psycholinguistic Abilities with culturally deprived children in the rural south. *Perceptual and Motor Skills*, 1970, *31*, 56-58.

Walker, D.K., Bane, M.M., & Bryk, A. *The quality of the Head Start planned variation data.* Cambridge, Mass.: Huron Institute, 1973.

Weber, C.U., Foster, P.F., & Weikart, D.P. An economic analysis of the Ypsilanti Perry Pre-school Project. *Monographs of the High/Scope Educational Research Foundation*, in press, No. 5.

Weikart, D.P., (Ed.). *Preschool intervention: Preliminary results of the Perry Preschool Project.* Ann Arbor, Mich.: Campus Publishers, 1967.

Weikart, D.P., Deloria, D., Lawser, S., & Wiegerink, R. Longitudinal results of the Ypsilanti Perry Preschool Project. *Monographs of the High/Scope Educational Research Foundation*, 1970, No. 1.

Weikart, D.P., Epstein, A.S., Schweinhart, L.J., & Bond, J.T. The Ypsilanti Preschool Curriculum Demonstration Project: Preschool years and longitudinal results. *Monographs of the High/Scope Educational Research Foundation*, 1978, No. 4.

Weikart, D.P., Rogers, L., Adcock, C., & McClelland, D. *The Cognitively Oriented Curriculum: A framework for preschool teachers.* Urbana: University of Illinois, 1971.

Weisberg, H.I. *Short-term cognitive effects of Head Start programs: A report on the third year of planned variation—1971-72.* Cambridge, Mass.: Huron Institute, 1974.

Wellman, B.L. IQ changes of preschool and nonpreschool groups during the preschool years: A summary of the literature. *Journal of Psychology*, 1945, *20*, 347-368.

Winer, B.J. *Statistical principles in experimental design.* New York: McGraw-Hill, 1962.

Wolf, R.M. *The identification and measurement of environmental process variables related to intelligence.* Unpublished doctoral dissertation, University of Chicago, 1964.

Zigler, E., Abelson, W.D., & Seitz, V. Motivational factors in the performance of economically disadvantaged children on the Peabody Picture Vocabulary Test. *Child Development*, 1973, *44*, 294-303.

Zigler, E., & Butterfield, E. Motivational aspects of changes in IQ test performance of culturally deprived nursery school children. *Child Development*, 1968, *39*, 1-14.

COMMENTARY BY ROBERT D. HESS
Lee L. Jacks Professor of Child Education
Stanford University

Educational research, unlike certain types of research in the physical and medical sciences, has few dramatic breakthroughs and, therefore, few surprises. The accumulation of knowledge is slow; the half-life of results of individual studies is often very short, and new data revise or contradict published findings. In educational research, persistence and patience are essential qualities.

This report is evidence that persistence pays off in evaluation research. It provides a formidable array of findings of the effectiveness of a preschool intervention program that was implemented in Ypsilanti, Michigan, from 1962 through 1967. The results show that intervention affected the school experience and success of children from the program during the first four grades. The report is impressive in the detail and care with which the design, sampling, testing, and data analysis are reported. The level of candor and of faithfulness in reporting give the reader the opportunity to decide what to make of the findings.

This report appears at a particularly appropriate time. There has been a half decade of debate about the usefulness of intervention programs with young children but this debate has led to little consensus. For a time, the interpretation of results of a national evaluation and the public statements of some child psychologists created the impression that intervention programs had been found to have no lasting impact. In the past two years, analysis and reanalysis of the follow-up results of a number of center and home-based studies began to challenge these conclusions as premature. The effect of these new findings is not yet clear for they are not entirely consistent with one another. But they seem to have two implications: they make the conclusions of "no impact" untenable at this point (or, at least, open to further examination), and they emphasize the need to assess the findings from a wide range of evaluation studies before drawing conclusions about what effect any intervention program has and whether some types of intervention are more effective than others.

The Perry Preschool Project and this report span an era that began in the late fifties and early sixties, through the mushrooming of national concern that led to Operation Head Start, and the waves of optimism and despair that came with the evaluations carried out during the post-Head Start years. The social changes in the U.S. during the past twenty years have brought to a new focus the issues of early education and child care. The report has particular implications for public policy about schooling and for the persisting issue of how preschool children can best be given care and experiences that prepare them for success in the schools.

This preschool program was one of the first to offer, in a formal fashion, school-related experiences to young children. It remains one of the few that concentrated on children whose performance on tests of mental functioning suggested that they would not do well in school. Weikart and his staff chose a difficult task. The level of knowledge about children from low-income backgrounds was extremely low; there were no models to follow and little by way of conceptual or theoretical structure to use in planning, except for the idea that intervention programs should be designed to enrich the environment of disadvantaged children.

It is astonishing and a little sobering to realize, fifteen years and many millions of dollars later, that most of the basic questions remain unanswered. Our best judgment, as professionals, is still largely grounded on professional bias.

Some knowledge about the effectiveness of early intervention programs is finally beginning to accumulate. Weikart and the staff of his Foundation have played a central role in providing useful evidence. In the early and mid-sixties, many preschool programs were initiated, but only a few have provided the field with evaluation data. Insistence on extensive, concurrent evaluation and on quality in the design and data analysis has been a mark of Weikart's work.

The study described in this report was planned in the early sixties when the practice and theory of evaluation had received little attention. This was before the outpouring of critiques, articles and books that began to state in a formal way the standard thought to be essential for sound assessment of program effectiveness. Despite the primitive nature of the field of evaluation at the time it was planned, the program described in the report included the basics: pretesting, a control group, assignment of children to experimental and control groups to minimize bias, posttesting, and follow-up testing. This evaluation thus qualifies as one with reliable results.

This study has another strength. It is not only a longitudinal investigation of the impact of intervention on a single group over time—it is a replicated longitudinal design. The report covers five different groups, each of which was followed through successive grades in the elementary school. Weikart has also collected follow-up data at later points, giving even more reliable evidence of the long term benefits of his Perry Preschool Program. For those who have not been involved in longitudinal research, it is difficult to recognize the enormous commitment of time, energy, and funds that are needed to gather data of this sort in a reliable way. The hazards were great: attrition of both staff and students, the possibility that instruments and concepts might become outmoded and inappropriate for use in follow-up studies, and the uncertainty of sustained funding. This study represents almost twenty years of planning, program execution, and evaluation. That in itself is a remarkable—and rare—achievement.

The effort has produced for Weikart, and for the field, a body of research data that will surely be an enduring resource. The multi-year, longitudinal design affords a stability of data that carries a special conviction. It deals with the possibility of fadeout of early cognitive gains in the only way that can be convincing.

Another strength of this evaluation is the use of multiple measures to assess the effects of the program and to provide indications of progress in different aspects of school-related behavior. The use of school success, as indicated by grade placement, is especially important for the group of children with which the program was concerned.

Although this study is remarkable in many ways, there are problems. One feature of the program on which some readers may want more detailed information is the curriculum itself and its evaluation during the five years. A pioneering effort of this kind required formative evaluation during the five years of intervention. The program for the last of the "waves" of the five years was perhaps not quite identical with that of the first year or two. At the time this program was developed, it would have been theoretically unwise, perhaps unethical, not to modify the curriculum and staff practices as experience suggested. This report does not, as a result, bear on the important issue of the differential effects, if any, of various kinds of intervention curricula and strategies.

The organization of the report is not always easy to follow. Reports of an evaluation as complex as this one are exceedingly difficult to prepare. There is a conflict between the need to keep the presentation within manageable bounds, in terms of detail of information and extent of technical material, and the need for full reporting of data gathering procedures and analysis of data. Our established and traditional formats for reporting complex and massive data are not adequate; new styles must be developed to accommodate the needs of the different sectors of the professional and evaluation community who will find selected, but different, aspects of the results of particular interest. This report is comprehensive, especially with its appendices, and is presented in a way that is comprehensive to various audiences with quite different professional training and interests.

The findings that Weikart and his staff report are provocative. They force us to push aside some of the simplistic and mechanistic notions of how early experience is processed by children and how it subsequently appears in modified behavior. The emphasis of many preschool programs for low-income children upon increasing intelligence, indicated by IQ test scores, was understandable given the state of the field in the early sixties. Weikart's report suggests, however, that while these test scores can be raised in the short run, they do not necessarily continue to show increments over control-group scores in follow-up comparisons. Nevertheless, the impact of the experience is positive, in traditional school terms, and sustained. It is reasonable to expect it to continue through schooling and into post-school functioning.

How did this happen? What are the linkages between these early experiences and later manifestations of competence in school?

The functional mechanism is apparently not an increase in general intelligence, in the sense of intellectual power. The IQ scores of the experimental groups drift toward the level of performance of the control groups and toward the experimental groups' own original pretest means. This gives little basis for assuming that the positive results come from a fundamental change in cognitive ability. The data do not invite alternative hypotheses. As Weikart and his colleagues suggest, the initial school experience of the experimental group may have been more successful than that of the children not in the program, giving them a sense of competence and confidence in their ability to deal with the demands of the classroom and the teacher. Perhaps this includes a willingness to approach the teacher, to get feedback about their work. Perhaps the preschool experience thus helped students acquire more quickly and successfully the role of pupil. If so, it supports the belief in the efficacy of motivational and social behavior in school performance.

Weikart's report has implications for several important issues. It shows that the impact of the program on children who participate results in financial savings to the school districts because of the lower number of children who are placed in special classes. The evaluation contributes to knowledge about long-term consequences of intervention and sets a standard for design of follow-up evaluations and for careful reporting of procedures and findings. There is an unusual opportunity to compare long-term trends with the picture that emerged from posttesting at the end of the intervention. This will lead many readers to doubt the results of any evaluation that is confined to posttest and immediate follow-up findings. For Weikart and for the field, persistence has been rewarded.

ROBERT D. HESS
STANFORD UNIVERSITY
AUGUST 23, 1977

COMMENTARY BY E. KUNO BELLER
Professor of Psychology
Temple University

"Those who have, get." This saying describes one of the major issues concerning preschool education for economically and educationally disadvantaged children. Throughout the century preschool education has been available and used by middle class parents and especially by academic and professional parents who lived in the vicinty of a University with Departments of Education and/or Home Economics. Although it was probably not the main concern of parents who enrolled their children in such nurseries to enrich the intellectual life and development of their children, many of the children attending these nurseries received a great deal of added stimulation because these nurseries were frequently associated with centers for graduate training in preschool education and laboratories for research in child development. The literature that emerged from such centers at the University of California at Berkeley, the University of Minnesota, the University of Iowa, the Fels Research Institute and others, between the First and Second World Wars attests to the "enrichment" that children received in the course of their attendance in nursery schools. The work at the Child Welfare Research Station of the University of Iowa was particularly productive in documenting the benefit that children received as a result of attending nursery school, although the issue of whether the nursery experience affected changes in IQ or academic achievement tended to overshadow the fact that children attending these nurseries benefited in a variety of ways from that experience. Most of the middle class children who had benefited from these nurseries, conducted by highly qualified staff with excellent supervision, moved on to elementary and high school systems which were equally qualified educationally to continue the early educational experience of these children.

Following the Second World War, another side of the school system and educational tract became visible and received increased attention. Just as the potential of preschool for enriched psychosocial and intellectual development was realized earlier, it now became evident that many schools in our nation became factories for failure, especially for children from low socio-economic backgrounds who had their first encounter with organized educational programs when they entered elementary school. In response to this realization, together with the "War on Poverty" during the mid 1960's, a large effort was mounted to counteract the educational disadvantages of poor children by offering them some educational experience prior to entering elementary school.

In contrast to the earlier preschool movement, which developed slowly over decades in the first half of the twentieth century, the new thrust in the form of Head Start represented an attempt to counteract, within a short time, the apparent reduced potential of lower class children for benefiting from universal education. While previously preschools offered high quality education and opportunities for careful research of its effects on development, the newly mounted national effort in the form of Head Start often lacked both quality education and an opportunity for documenting through careful research the impact of its efforts on the children it served. This posed a dilemma because the justification and financing of the new Head Start facilities for deprived children were quickly challenged. In sharp contrast to the preschool movement which continued without being questioned, Head Start was attacked on a wide front for a variety of reasons. The intellectual and scientific basis of criticism was spearheaded by Arthur Jensen on racial grounds and on the basis of hereditary inferiority of black, as well as poor, children. Others criticized the Head Start efforts as an attempt of the majority culture to impose middle class white values on children whose families adhered to a different set of values. Last but not least, the wisdom of the financial investment in Head Start was challenged on the basis of questioning its cost effectiveness.

In spite of the urgency of these questions and regardless of their scientific, social and financial merit the organization of Head Start and the nature of the educational programs it offered to deprived children made it extremely difficult, if not impossible, to mount an effort towards objective and scientific evaluation of its effect on disadvantaged children. A dramatic example of this impossibility has been the ill-fated Westinghouse Study which had more political than scientific value in its design and conclusions. The reasons for the extreme difficulties of researching the effects of Head Start were, among others, that the same forces that questioned its justification as an educational effort were disinclined to provide the financial support necessary to set up national studies which would provide objective evidence of the impact of Head Start on children. Such an evaluation would require the establishment of a baseline of children entering Head Start in order to determine change due to their Head Start experience, the provision and replication of quality programs and employment of control groups. Even today, a decade after the demand for evaluation has been raised publicly, these prerequisites are not being met on a nationwide basis.

Fortunately there have been a few programs which started in the early 60's that had the courage and wisdom to make a supreme effort to meet the basic criteria for evaluating the short and long range effects of quality education on deprived lower class children. The study reported in this monograph represents a pioneer effort which undertook to apply those criteria which are necessary for an objective and scientific evaluation of what Head Start *could* do. Precisely that is the important question to ask. The wisdom and justification for providing early education to socially and economically deprived children should not be judged from poorly controlled investigations of Head Start programs with an unknown educational quality.

Only a quality program carried out over a long enough period of time whose effect on children is studied over a number of years as they move through the public school system can address the question as to whether the expense required for educational preschool programs for deprived lower class children can be justified. The study reported in this monograph offers an opportunity to evaluate evidence in response to the question: "Can preschool education change the academic motivation and achievement of deprived children as they move through the school system? Can such an effort break, or at least weaken the vicious cycle of disadvantage for an appreciable number of children?" The presence of unbiased control groups, the assessment of baseline measures, the offering of a quality educational program, the replication of both the program and its evaluation, and the long term follow-up of the children through the school system make the outcome of this study invaluable as empirical evidence of what Head Start could do for deprived lower class children.

A further value of this study is that it used multiple criteria for measuring change and the effect of the preschool experience on the children. Multiple criteria permitted the investigators to examine interacting factors of the school experience. The reciprocal nature of these interactions suggested by the authors in their discussion of the findings is particularly important for avoiding oversimplification of conclusions and effective planning of future preschool programs and research. The positive and negative cycles that improved academic achievement sets up in the child's interactions with his teachers has been documented empirically in previous research.[1] This writer found that teachers react more positively to children who perform well academically and vice versa. A positive feedback system emerges between teachers and children. The positive response of the children to the teachers' efforts is not limited to their improved academic performance. Children who succeed academically show greater concern for the teachers' needs: e.g., when the teacher cannot respond to their request immediately these children either wait patiently or try to carry out the task by themselves or busy themselves with some other activity. The opposite pattern has been found for children who fail academically. Their teachers give them less positive attention, respond less readily to their requests, while the children themselves resort more readily to negative attention seeking and disturbing behavior when their requests are not met immediately by

[1] Beller, E.K. Environmental reciprocity: A socio-emotional view of development. In K. Riegel & J. Meacham (Eds.), *The developing individual in a changing world.* The Hague Mouton Press, 1976.

their teachers. The suggestion of the authors that similar vicious cycles exist between academic failure, negative social behavior and assignment to special education classes as well as retention rate, points to the same type of pattern. These patterns of reciprocal interactions are critical for an understanding of our urban schools as factories of failure for children who enter with lowered probability for academic success.

An important part of this pattern is the lack of mutual support between home and school. As the authors have pointed out, close contact between teachers and parents gives the teacher an opportunity to adapt her educational method to the individual needs of the child. Once more this suggested relationship is corroborated by earlier findings.[2] Head Start teachers who showed a greater interest in the child's parents and who were more concerned with the individual needs of children produced more children who gained from Head Start than other teachers.

Finally, the care with which the authors have described the nature of their successful program should contribute much to planning of future preschool programs for poverty children. The time teachers were given for planning their daily program, the continual evaluation and re-evaluation of daily educational efforts and the closeness of the educational team to their research evaluators are invaluable information. What emerges is the impression of a highly engaged educational team which produced something like a concerned society for the growing child. It is as though the intense effort of these investigators has created a learning ecology for children of poverty which has accomplished preventively what much costlier efforts to correct later on cannot accomplish. The preventive work, however, is not presented as an inoculation against failure. The authors have shown vividly how the earlier preventive steps produce their own dynamism in the form of positive cycles carried by feedback systems between academic achievement, socially adjustive behavior of pupils and teacher facilitation in promoting the children rather than marking them as failures through retention and assignment to special education classes for learning disabilities or unmanageable behavior patterns. In sum, the results of this study make the continuation of the work that produced them a matter of great urgency.

E. KUNO BELLER
TEMPLE UNIVERSITY
APRIL 3, 1978

[2] Beller, E.K. Teaching styles and their effects on problem-solving behavior in Head Start programs. In E. Grotberg (Ed.), Critical issues in research related to disadvantaged children. Princeton, N.J.: Educational Testing Service, 1968.